P9-DEC-701

Twayne's United States Authors Series

SYLVIA E. BOWMAN, *Editor*

INDIANA UNIVERSITY

John Fox, Jr.

JOHN FOX, JR.

By WARREN I. TITUS

George Peabody College for Teachers

 174

Twayne Publishers, Inc.   ::   New York

For
Judy, John, and Jan

Preface

"IT IS DIFFICULT to review John Fox's work so as to convey any just idea of it in either substance or form," wrote Fox's friend, Thomas Nelson Page, in 1919. "His work was of the kind which no description can present. To get any conception of it, it must be read."[1] Yet, Fox's books are largely unread today—except possibly by juveniles—and are deemed no more than jejune period pieces illustrating how susceptible our fathers were to mawkish sentimentality. At least two of his novels, *The Little Shepherd of Kingdom Come* and *The Trail of the Lonesome Pine,* two of the most popular books ever published in American literature, are still in print; and, if the reader can overlook the typical Romantic strains characteristic of the time in which they were written, he may find an occasional glimpse of a region and of a people that has the stamp of authenticity. Even more, in half a dozen long-forgotten stories—better works, really, than his best-selling novels—Fox left a useful portrait of the life of the Southern mountaineer that presaged the work of twentieth-century historians, folklorists, and linguists. Scarcely more than a competent second-rate writer on the whole, Fox nevertheless bequeathed to those who read him a legacy of local-color lore that should not be forgotten.

The purpose of this study is to achieve four things: (1) to give a brief, though by no means definitive, biography of John Fox, Jr.; (2) to recall to the minds of those who have read him, and to bring to those who have not, the basic content of his several books and stories; (3) to give some hint of his contemporary reception as a popular best-selling writer; and (4), most important, to make some critical assessment of his individual writings and of his work as a whole. To accomplish these objectives, it has been necessary, among other things, to follow Page's advice to read or reread all of Fox's writing. In the case of the popular novels, this proved, frankly, to be a rather dreary assignment; for the fictional tastes of 1903 and 1908 are not those of today. But for much of his short story writing—particularly in his earliest period—the assignment provided a pleasant and rewarding surprise. There is a small quantity of Fox's work—perhaps a half-dozen sketches—that bears comparison with the best that any of the local colorists in American fiction produced. If more readers knew the *Hell-fer-Sartain* sketches and if fewer passed their judgments on the basis of *The Little Shepherd of Kingdom Come* or *The Trail of the Lonesome Pine*, Fox would fare better when the literary histories are written.

Pursuing Fox's career has sent me to several repositories for both published and unpublished information. The largest body of Fox materials is in the University of Kentucky Library at Lexington. My special thanks go to Dr. Jacqueline Bull, Director of Special Collections, and to her efficient staff at the Kentucky library for making these materials available to me. Mrs. Basil Hayden, hostess at the Duncan Tavern Historic Center in Paris, Kentucky, was most helpful in giving me access to the many Fox items in the John Fox, Jr., Memorial Library Room of the tavern. And at the Clifton Waller Barrett Library of the University of Virginia Library in Charlottesville, other Fox letters—primarily from Fox to a Harvard classmate, Micajah Fible—were placed at my disposal by Mr. Robert Stocking, Curator of Manuscripts, whose assistance is gratefully acknowledged. Other libraries that hold Fox materials—particularly letters—kindly provided photostats of everything requested. A listing of the specific sources of such materials is included in the Selected Bibliography.

Particular mention should be made of my delightful conversations with Mrs. Elizabeth Fox Moore, sister of the novelist, a charming lady who still lives in John Fox's home at Big Stone Gap, Virginia. I am doubly grateful to Mrs. Moore for furnishing those choice bits of information that only a sister could provide as well as granting permission to use and quote from her brother's letters. Hostesses at the June Tolliver House in Big Stone Gap were also helpful in providing background materials and in sharing with me their recollections of the author whom some of them had known personally.

I wish to express my appreciation to the American Philosophical Society for a grant from its Penrose Fund which provided the financial means for much of the research that went into the present study. And I also wish to thank Professor Sylvia E. Bowman, Editor of Twayne's United States Authors Series, and Professor Oscar Cargill, retired chairman of the All-University English Department, New York University, and an ever obliging friend, for their perceptive and helpful suggestions in the preparation of the manuscript. Neither is responsible for any of the book's shortcomings, but both contributed to whatever value it may have.

Grateful acknowledgment is made to Charles Scribner's Sons for permission to use quotations from copyrighted works of John Fox, Jr.

Warren I. Titus

Nashville, Tennessee
April, 1969

Contents

Chronology

1862   John William Fox, Jr., born December 16 at Stony Point (near Paris), Bourbon County, Kentucky; oldest son of John W. Fox, Sr., and his second wife, Minerva Carr Fox.

1867   Entered his father's school, Stony Point Academy.

1875   Gave the salutatory and a declamation on "Napoleon and the Battle of Warsaw" at June exhibition ceremonies of his father's school.

1878   Went to Lexington to study privately under his older half-brother, James, a recent graduate of Kentucky University (Transylvania). Took Harvard examinations in June and received his certificate of entrance to the Harvard freshman class, but financial reverses forced his father into bankruptcy that summer and Fox was unable to enter Harvard. Entered Kentucky University in the fall. Met and studied under James Lane Allen.

1880   One of the speakers at the exhibition of the Periclean Society at Kentucky University. Took and passed examinations for Harvard once again in the summer. In September entered Harvard sophomore class at age seventeen years and nine months.

1881   James Fox embarked on coal-mining enterprises at Jellico, Tennessee.

1882   Home from Harvard in the summer, Fox went to Jellico to work in his brother's mines. First introduction to mountain people and their ways. Returned to Harvard for senior year in the fall.

1883   Graduated *cum laude* from Harvard, June 21, youngest member of his class. Went to New York; eventually worked for New York *Sun* until fall. Entered Columbia University Law School in September; dropped out in December.

1884   Reporter for the New York *Times* on an assignment basis. First met Thomas Nelson Page, a lifelong friend.

1885   Returned to Paris, Kentucky, in February because of ill-health; convalesced through spring and summer.

1886   Worked in mines at Jellico again for a time. Taught in his father's school and tutored privately.

1888   Continued teaching and tutoring sons of wealthy patrons. Spent another summer in the mountains of eastern Kentucky. Began writing his story, "A Mountain Europa." Fox brothers, James and Horace, moved their mining engineering operations to Big Stone Gap, Virginia.

1889   Went into partnership with his half-brother, James, and his brother, Horace, in the real estate business at Big Stone Gap. Made contacts with wealthy friends in Louisville and in the East for land investments at the Gap.

1890   John Fox, Sr., and rest of family moved to Big Stone Gap in April. Fox brothers actively engaged in mining and boom development. Joined volunteer police force, a local vigilante group, to bring order to the area. Made Big Stone Gap his permanent home until his death.

1892   As a member of volunteer police force, Fox participated in hanging of Talt Hall. First story, "A Mountain Europa," published in *Century* in September.

1893   Economic collapse at Big Stone Gap. Turned in earnest to writing, lecturing, and public reading.

1894   Went on the lyceum circuit through the East and South for the next few years under managements of Major J. B. Pond and Southern Lyceum Bureau. Met Theodore Roosevelt for first time.

1895   First book published, *A Cumberland Vendetta and Other Stories*.

1897   *Hell-fer-Sartain and Other Stories* published in June; *The Kentuckians* in December.

1898   Went as *Harper's* correspondent to Cuba in Spanish-American War.

1899   Elected to membership in National Institute of Arts and Letters.

1900   *Crittenden.*

1901   *Blue-grass and Rhododendron.*

1903   *The Little Shepherd of Kingdom Come,* his first best seller, published.

1904   Went as *Scribner's* correspondent to Japan and Manchuria to report Russo-Japanese War. Honorary Master of Arts degree from Kentucky University. *Christmas-Eve on Lonesome and Other Stories* published.

1905 *Following the Sun Flag.*

1906 *A Knight of the Cumberland.*

1908 *The Trail of the Lonesome Pine,* his second best seller, published. Lived in New York several months of each year during this time. Married Fritzi Scheff, comic opera star, December 13.

1912 January 29, *The Trail of the Lonesome Pine,* adapted by Eugene Walter from the novel by Fox, opened at the New Amsterdam Theater, New York, starring Charlotte Walker and W. S. Hart. First of several successful runs. John Fox, Sr., died in June.

1913 Divorced from Fritzi Scheff in February. *The Heart of the Hills* published in March. Went to Palm Beach and Aiken, South Carolina, for the winter and to the West on a hunting trip in the fall.

1914 Made first trip to Europe in February and March.

1915 Experienced difficulties over dramatization of *The Little Shepherd of Kingdom Come.*

1916 First filming of *The Trail of the Lonesome Pine.* Two other movie versions, one in 1922, the other in 1936, were to follow.

1917 *In Happy Valley.*

1919 Died July 8 at Big Stone Gap. Buried at Paris, Kentucky.

1920 *Erskine Dale—Pioneer* completed by sister and published posthumously.

CHAPTER 1

The Early Years

JOHN FOX, JR., loved Kentucky. "The land seems in all the New World, to have been the pet shrine of the Great Mother herself," he wrote in *The Little Shepherd of Kingdom Come*.[1] Elsewhere his novels and stories abound in exuberant celebrations of the bluegrass region in particular and of the state in general. Though he lived much of his adult life—particularly his life as an author—in Virginia, he always considered Kentucky his home. And it was at his expressed wish that he was brought to Kentucky in death in 1919.

I *Ancestry and Childhood*

Fox's ancestors had been in Kentucky for generations, largely in Fayette and Clark counties. His mother was Minerva Carr, daughter of William Carr and Elizabeth Clary, and sister of Ollie Carr, a noted nineteenth-century minister of the Christian Church; and both the Carr and Clary families had had roots in Kentucky for many years. On his father's side, a lineage Fox knew more about, his ancestors had migrated from Virginia about 1790, crossing through Cumberland Gap over the Wilderness Road. One intrepid forebear, Fox's great-great-grandmother, Mary Conrad Fox, crossed on the Wilderness Road as a widow with seven children. In *Erskine Dale—Pioneer*, Fox retold the adventures of some of these hardy pioneer ancestors as he had pieced their story together.[2]

John William Fox, the author's father, was himself a remarkable man—a schoolmaster and a scholar of no small accomplishments for his day. On a schoolmaster's pay, this hardy soul managed to support and educate ten children, eight boys and two girls, in the finest Classical tradition of that era. All of the children turned out well—three were Harvard graduates, one became a doctor, and two were engineers. The father lived until 1912, an active source of strength to his large family until very near the end of his life.

John William Fox was twice married—the first time to Kitty Rice in 1852. This marriage ended with her death in childbirth in June, 1860. Three boys, James, Sidney, and Everett, were born to the couple. The senior Fox married again early in 1862— this time to Minerva Carr of Mayslick, Kentucky. The first child born to Minerva Carr and John William Fox was John, Jr., on December 16, 1862. Four more boys and two girls followed. A large family, it was a happy and, above all, a closely knit one. John was as close to his half-brothers—even closer in the case of James—as he was to his full brothers and sisters. The family worked and played together and kept close personal touch with one another throughout their lives.

All the Fox children were born at Stony Point, a small farm community about eight miles south of Paris, Kentucky, on the road from Paris to Winchester. Fox grew up at Stony Point and Paris in Bourbon County, the heart of Kentucky's famed bluegrass section. His father's academy, Stony Point Academy, was a private boarding school for boys and girls; and there John, like all the children, received his early education. The regimen, from all accounts, was firm and thorough. He was well grounded in the Classics, for his father was a firm believer in the Classical curriculum.

But life was not all school either, even as the son of a schoolmaster. Young John Fox and his brothers loved to hunt and fish, and they often took long walks through the fields and woods. The senior Fox, who was interested in all forms of plant life, regularly made botanical collections of specimens found in the immediate area. The father bequeathed his interest to at least two of his sons, James and John, Jr., who avidly studied and loved the flowers and plants of the Paris fields.[3] Later, John participated in the summertime activity of his father and older brothers in collecting grass seed from the farms of the bluegrass which they then sold in Lexington—only one of the means the father had of supplementing his income. John Fox, Sr., also learned surveying and, again in the company of his sons, frequently spent the summer months hiring himself out on surveying expeditions in the area.

In 1878, young John went to Lexington, Kentucky, to study

with his older half-brother James, who had graduated from Kentucky University (now Transylvania University) two years earlier and was teaching in Lexington. His brother James—perhaps the greatest single .influence on John, at least during his formative years—was a bright young man who might well have attended Harvard himself and achieved literary honors. As it was, he went into business enterprise and, with hard work and shrewdness, made a mark in the industrial world as an entrepreneur and investor. In 1878, however, James was following his father's profession as a schoolteacher. And he made an ideal tutor for John, for soon the younger brother was also enrolled in Kentucky University where he took up the study of Homer, Xenophon, Virgil, and Livy, together with solid geometry, analytical trigonometry, analytical geometry, and algebra. "John, Jr. has his studies arranged and is doing good work," James wrote the elder Fox in September, 1879. "He will be well prepared to enter the Harvard sophomore class next September. John is a sharp boy, diligent student, and I believe is the coming member of the family, for he will certainly make his mark. As you say, he writes an interesting letter, and as I can add, he does everything well whether it be work or recreation."[4]

John was indeed applying himself well. He always seemed to recognize, as did all the Fox children, the great value of an education—another debt owed, no doubt, to the example of the fine father. "Give me an education," John wrote in 1880, "and I will ask a penny of no one; and an education I am determined to have if patience and perseverance can accomplish it."[5]

As early as 1878, John had taken the examinations to enter Harvard College. He passed and would have been eligible to enter the college as a freshman that year, but his father's fortunes were at a low ebb that summer (he had to go into bankruptcy) and so John went instead to Kentucky University. In 1880, he took the examinations for Harvard again and left for Cambridge that fall to enter the sophomore class. He was seventeen years and nine months old at the time.

II   *Harvard College*

John Fox's trip east to Harvard in the autumn of 1880 was the first traveling he had done beyond the confines of his native state. His excitement in encountering the attractions of New

York City was communicated in a letter written to his brother
James in October:

> I soon got the run of the streets and could go anywhere by myself.
> Walked up and down the Bowery several times; went into a 10¢ show
> and saw the learned pig, Captain Jack's daughter, the Circassian girl,
> Albino, etc. Was taken in completely on that. Went down Fifth Avenue
> and saw the palatial residences of the rich nabobs. Especially admired
> Stewart's residence and business house which (the latter) I went
> through. Walked down Broadway, and ran across the street several
> times to see if I could perform that feat without getting run over.
> Followed Broadway down to Old Trinity Church. Climbed up the
> stairway and obtained a splendid view of New York, Jersey City, and
> Brooklyn. I then took a seat in the church to look at it closely.
> Someone, a master hand, was playing on an organ.[6]

The sentiments in the letter were portentous of the lures of the
theatrical, musical, and literary phases of New York life that Fox
the writer was to find so appealing in the future.

John's Harvard career was a success from beginning to end.
He elected Latin, Greek, Italian, French, and English at the
college. (He was the only one of the new candidates who passed
his Latin examination successfully.) Because of conflicts in hours
of recitations and examinations, he took what he liked at first;
and his choice was significant. He also became interested in
amateur athletics at Harvard, although his health had never been
robust; all his life he was a spare, sinewy man whose appearance
suggested a delicate constitution. At Harvard he attempted to
overcome his frailties by taking daily exercise in the gymnasium.
"Am now learning to turn somersaults in the air, handsprings
and all sorts of didoes," he proudly wrote home in October, 1880.
He noted that, while he intended to study diligently, he was not
going to ruin his health in the classroom: "I would rather stand
moderate and have a deep broad chest, strong muscles and an
amazing appetite and in all probability live twenty years longer."[7]
His letters during his Harvard days indicated his pride in his
newly developed muscles and his new freedom from headaches
and catarrh that had plagued him earlier.

Harvard also meant a new social life. At first, he was lonely
in Cambridge; for there were not many Southerners there at
the time—fewer still from Kentucky. But, eventually, he found
companionship and joined the social clubs and fun groups. During the year of 1881-82 he lived at Thayer Hall in the college

Yard, and here his associations with his fellow students increased. He had studied music before he left Kentucky, and now this interest—plus others in dramatics and oratory—came to the fore. He entered into college theatricals and played the end man in at least one minstrel performance at Harvard. "It is much nicer here this year than it was last year as there are about ten Kentucky fellows now," he noted in 1882.[8]

Perhaps the acme of his college dramatic career was reached when he played a woman's part in a production of *Papa Perrichon*. Fox was assigned the role because of his soft features and his capacities to perform any acting assignment given him. During the early summer of 1882 the boys took the play on tour to Exeter, Portland, Bangor, and Augusta, Maine. Although the play was a financial loss, Fox gained fun and experience from it. Indeed, he toyed for a time with the idea of making a career of the stage while he was still at Harvard. Though he later gave up the idea, his stage career in college served him later when he became one of the most accomplished and celebrated platform readers of his own works.

III *New York and Journalism*

Fox graduated *cum laude* from Harvard in June, 1883. He used to say that, when he graduated, he knew more Latin and Greek than he did English. Perhaps his Classical training turned him toward the law; or perhaps it was his Southern heritage. At any rate, he went immediately after graduation to New York City to prepare to enter Columbia Law School in the fall. His brother Sidney, who was practicing medicine in Brooklyn at the time, wrote that he felt John could secure an income by tutoring young men for college and could get into a law office to learn some practical aspects of the trade before entering law school in September.

Fox found on arrival in New York, however, that he could not find either pupils or a law position. So he turned to journalism, another career that had suggested itself to him during his last months at Harvard. He secured a position as a reporter with the New York *Sun*, but his connection was not a permanent or a full-time one. Rather, he was sent on special assignments. Nevertheless, he was elated at the prospects of his fifteen-dollar-a-week job, which, along with the prodding of his family (specifically, his father and older brother James), kept him in New York until he entered the Columbia Law School in the fall of 1883.

That his interests were not altogether with the law is evidenced by a letter he wrote his mother on November 10, 1883, after he had started his classes at Columbia. He said that he and Buckner Allen, an old Kentucky friend, were writing a play together: "So if you hear through the papers that a new play is to be brought out soon in New York written by the talented young dramatists, Messrs. Allen and Fox, you may know that means your humble son and servant. We are going to do it. There will be fame yet in the Fox family."[9] The play came to nought, of course; and Fox's law career fared no better. He did not care enough for the lectures at Columbia to continue beyond December. Actually, he was never very much excited about the legal profession, but in the 1880's it was the usual field for a Southern Bourbon to pursue. His father, for one, must have considered it far more attractive for his son than anything John was currently contemplating. But John Fox was not one to be bound to a career by custom or inheritance.

For the time being, he still flirted with journalism, although his experiences with the *Sun* had not been truly successful. "As a reporter I was a failure," he said.[10] Years later, talking to the editor of the *Sun*, he said that he had never really recovered from the months spent on the paper. The paper, the editor smilingly replied, had not recovered either. Nevertheless, early in 1884 Fox took a part-time position on the New York *Times*. Once again, he was on assignment, not on a regular working basis. "Last week my salary was $26.00," he wrote in May, 1884.[11] He gained an entree into some of the club life of New York and also reported activities on the Bowery and at the beaches: "On Sundays the editor very kindly sends me away to some watering resort where I spend a very enjoyable, if a little lonesome, day and then write up a short pretty little description of it."[12] Occasionally, he was summoned to more unsavory assignments in the police department. But, though his early interest in the various phases of New York life was undoubtedly assuaged by such reportorial assignments, his health soon broke under the rigors of the tasks.

Late in the summer of 1884 Fox came home for vacation to Stony Point. He was to return to New York again briefly for his newspaper career, but in truth his excursion into journalism had ended. His health was so broken by the spring of 1885 that he was forced back to Kentucky under doctor's orders once more to recuperate. He never returned to the newspaper field again. But the time had not been wasted: experience on the New York papers had initiated him to the world of writing, had made him a more acute observer of life, and had given him the opportunity to get his name into print. He had written a few editorial pieces and some feature articles while on the *Times*, though these were not enough to get him very well known by the public. Perhaps of more importance, he made the acquaintance of some wealthy, socially prominent people in the city—connections renewed when he had achieved new and more secure fame as a writer.

IV *Mining in the Mountains*

John W. Fox, Sr., worked hard all his life to secure for his sons the advantages of a superior education. As a result, the Fox sons always had a great sense of their debt to their father. Part of the driving ambition of their lives was the attempt to repay their own obligations and to help their father gain some respite from his active life in his late years. Opportunity to meet these objectives seemed to be present when John Fox, Jr., returned to Kentucky in 1885.

In 1881, James Fox had embarked in land speculation and mineral development in the mountain regions near the Kentucky-Tennessee-Virginia borders. This section of the country, long isolated because of its inaccessibility to transportation and the rugged terrain that encompassed it, was in the midst of a rapidly booming mineral exploitation. The coal wealth of the Cumberlands was being tapped by Eastern and English capital, and many venturesome young men were plunging into the business of opening up the country and mining its mineral resources.

John Proctor, a business acquaintance in Lexington, and other friends had encouraged James Fox to get in on the ground floor of these mining ventures. As a result, James went in 1881 to Jellico, Tennessee, near the Kentucky border, to engage in the coal business; his brother Horace joined him there a few months later. John, Jr., had followed his brothers to the mountain region during the summer of 1882 while he was home from Harvard. During July and August of that year he had his first introduction to the mountain people and their ways at Jellico; and he was fascinated. Already his brother James was suggesting that John

become a writer; and, lending encouragement at every opportunity, he urged John to write of the mountain regions, sensing
that this was a new area for literary exploitation. When John
returned from New York in 1885, therefore, he went once
again to the mining area of southeastern Kentucky after a few
weeks spent in recuperation at his home in Paris. Soon he was
assisting his brothers in their engineering endeavors; the work was
rugged, but it was in the out-of-doors. And it gave him further
opportunity to learn the mountain people and the mountain life.

About this time Fox apparently began to think more seriously
about a literary career, although he had entertained the idea off
and on since Harvard days. For the next four or five years he
ventured back and forth between the mountains of Kentucky,
the bluegrass region, and New York. Journalism was pretty
much out of his thoughts. Occasionally, he taught for brief
periods in and around Paris or tutored the sons of wealthy
friends, sometimes traveling with them as they went south to
Florida or Georgia for the winter. There was always the alluring
prospect of a fortune in the Jellico mines; many were now convinced of this possibility. But Fox's interest was toward a different use of the area, as an 1887 letter to a Louisville friend,
Micajah Fible, indicates. "I am drinking in like a sponge the peculiar life, the peculiar ideas of this peculiar mountain-race and
its beautiful natural environment," he wrote from Jellico. "I rise
at 5, dine at 12, sup at 5:30 and go to bed before 9. I work in
the office with the books, study all the departments during the
day, write letters, scribble conversational bits, vernacular idio-
syncracies, in my note-book and work a little, a very little, on
a hopeless and unsatisfactory story."[13]

What the story may have been we cannot know, but it is
possible to speculate that he was still engaged in constructing
a mountain tale based on an incident earlier told him by his
brother. James Lane Allen, whom he had met in his school
days at Lexington and who had added his encouragement to that
of James, suggested that Fox send the completed story to the
Century magazine. Finally, after several months of intermittent
work on "A Mountain Europa," as Fox was calling the story,
he did send the manuscript to the *Century* in 1890. The reply
from Richard Watson Gilder, the magazine's editor, was generally
favorable:

Although the general situation of your story "A Mountain Europa" is somewhat hackneyed, it interests us a good deal. The greatest fault, to our minds, is a certain "wordiness" which pervades almost the entire narrative. The style is dignified, but it is rather conventional and over-stately in expression. We think you would greatly strengthen the story if you would go over it carefully, condensing nearly every page to its most valuable points. If you would kindly do this in colored ink or pencil, and would send the story back to us, we should be glad to use it.[14]

Fox might have taken this reception to his first serious story quite happily; actually, he seems to have been chagrined by Gilder's criticism. He noted the contents of the letter to James Lane Allen, who responded as a kindly mentor should:

You might as well learn at once that a letter from an editor never pleased anybody altogether. . . . From everything in this letter it seems to me you should learn something. The "wordiness" complained of is what I warned you of as systematizing your ideas—grouping and shading them around what is styled "the most valuable points." When the little ideas are set around the larger ones, as little gems around larger gems, definitely, deliberately, for the working out and enriching of a well conceived and well understood plan, I am confident that for *you* wordiness will disappear. Your mind is not naturally a wordy mind—except when you speak with embarrassment of love![15]

The revised story was finally accepted, and Fox was launched on his literary career as an interpreter of Kentucky mountain life.

CHAPTER 2

Exploiting the Mountains

I *"A Mountain Europa"*

"**A** MOUNTAIN Europa," Fox's first story of consequence, was the first of many he was to write making use of the Kentucky mountain locale; and it was to have a long publishing history.[1] It appeared serially first in *Century* magazine for September and October of 1892. A book edition was published by Harper and Brothers in 1899, although the story was scarcely more than a novelette. Scribner's, who became Fox's publishers after 1900, brought out new editions in 1904 and 1914; and it also appeared in the collection *A Cumberland Vendetta and Other Stories* published by Harper's in 1895 and 1900 and by Scribner's in 1904 and 1918. Few writers have had as successful an initial effort as Fox.

The setting for the story is the Jellico mining camp area along the Tennessee-Kentucky border to which the Fox brothers had been introduced in their recent ventures. Clayton, a sophisticated young Easterner (patterned ever so slightly after Fox himself), comes to the Jellico region from the scholarly pursuits of German university life. His parents, victims of a current financial depression, have summoned their son home to investigate the possibilities in some mineral lands purchased some years earlier in the Southern mountains. Expecting the worst in the new environment, Clayton finds instead that he is intrigued by the new life and "suffer [s] less than he anticipated."[2] He is immediately drawn by the beauty of the hills and the charm of the mountaineers. On one of his many walking excursions into the mountains, he meets a young girl riding a bull along a mountain path. Startled by such a sight, though later assured by a friend that it is a common occurrence for women in the mountains to ride bulls or oxen, he conjures up the Classic image of Europa.

The young girl has a quaint, subdued charm that attracts him, and he determines to learn more about her and her life.

Through a mountaineer friend, Uncle Tommy Brooks, Clayton discovers that the girl is Easter Hicks, daughter of a moonshiner and suspected murderer, Bill Hicks. Hicks has taken to hiding in the mountains to escape the law; his wife and daughter have remained at the mountain cabin to provide whatever contact he can brook with the outside world. Uncle Tommy reports also that Sherd Raines, a mountain preacher, has interested himself in Easter and that matrimony is a likely possibility.

At this point, however, Clayton has no thought of a love affair with the girl. He is simply drawn to the mountain beauty— a rare flower in the midst of otherwise rather drab people. He comes to the girl's cabin, meets the mother, and gradually wins the girl's confidence. He sees possibilities for intellectual development in the girl and proceeds to tutor her so that she may be made more aware of the world and of the education necessary to succeed in it. Gradually, as we might suspect, he falls in love with her, and she with him.

At about this point, he is summoned home to the East by his family. There he comes to believe his relationship with Easter is futile; he realizes the difficulty of fitting her into the kind of life he and his family have envisioned for him. He is almost persuaded not to return; but he finally does—and fortunately for Easter, for she has by now wholeheartedly committed herself to him.

Clayton returns to the mountains determined to marry the girl and to take her forth into the world where he is hopeful she can learn to adjust to the ways of his society and finally to fit into the life he will lead. A wedding is arranged despite some objections from the father, Bill Hicks, who regards all outsiders as "furriners" and enemies. Hicks is persuaded finally to accept the idea of his daughter marrying an outsider; but, at the wedding celebration, he becomes drunk and all his uncouthness is brought to the fore. Sherd Raines, who has befriended young Clayton when he realizes his intentions are serious and who has enough regard for Easter to honor her choice, attempts, without success, to subdue Hicks. Hicks picks up a gun, fires at "furriner" Clayton in a blind rage, and hits his daughter Easter who steps into the line of fire perhaps to save Clayton, perhaps to grasp the gun from her father's hands. The shot is fatal; Easter dies before another morning.

The story ends with Clayton and Sherd walking down the mountain: Sherd, to continue his religious ventures in the hills; Clayton, to return to the Eastern city civilization from which he has come. "Thar seems to be a penalty for lovin' too much down hyar," Sherd philosophizes; "n'I reckon that both of us hev got hit to pay."[3]

The plot, of course, is melodramatic, though not wholly incredible, and certainly not so incongruous as a later reviewer for the *Nation* was to find it.[4] The characters are not very convincingly drawn; the story is too short for that. Clayton's whole attitude seems unreal, and he is apparently a foil for Fox to introduce the various mountain types—preacher, mountaineer mother, moonshiner, pure mountain girl, feudsman—that he wishes to record. The mountain characters are indeed better delineated than Clayton, but they, too, lack substance and seem more shadowy than real. Two exceptions are Uncle Tommy Brooks, a witty, homespun mountaineer-philosopher, and Sherd Raines, the circuit rider. Somewhat reminiscent of Morton Goodwin in Edward Eggleston's *The Circuit Rider*, Raines is as good a portrait of the Southern mountain preacher as can be found anywhere in the pages of fictional local color. Fox was to introduce him again in later stories, just as he was to employ the Uncle Tommy Brooks type for humorous effect in subsequent sketches.

The descriptions of the mountain landscapes and the atmosphere of the hill country are the strong features of the novelette. Fox could always do good work in descriptive passages, and his first story contains some of his best lines depicting mountain scenery and suggesting the moods of the mountaineer society. The opening and closing scenes of the story are particularly effective. A comparison with Mary Noailles Murfree, who had earlier written of the Southern mountaineer, is to Fox's advantage as far as description is concerned. Although Fox lacked her character analysis, he equalled and sometimes surpassed her in expository prose. The dialect is also good—and there is just enough to seem realistic; not enough to cloy, as it sometimes does in Miss Murfree's stories.

In this first story of the mountaineers, Fox found the theme he was to employ again and again in his mountain fiction—the clash of the outside world with the mountaineer society occasioned by the mineral exploitation of the late nineteenth century. The usual pattern in this fiction is to have an educated, gentlemanly outsider—most often a geologist, engineer, or teacher—come into the mountain community and there meet an unlettered, unmannered, but naturally well-endowed young mountain girl; to have them fall in love with each other; and to record the problems that such a love poses because of their contrasting backgrounds. Sometimes, as in *The Trail of the Lonesome Pine*, the problems are overcome and the match made. More often, as in *The Heart of the Hills* or in "A Mountain Europa," the difficulties are insurmountable; the story ends without the marriage of the lovers.

"A Mountain Europa" also indicated Fox's interest in the mountaineer's history and code. For almost thirty years he was to compile a sociological record of Cumberland mountain life in his fiction. That this mountain life was a part of the contemporary scene representative of the American pioneer ideal and that it was about to pass away by the end of the nineteenth century seemed to him a message worth recording. Clayton speculates in the story on the "gaunt mountaineer stalking awkwardly in the rear of the march toward civilization":

Gradually it had dawned upon him that this last, silent figure, traced through Virginia, was closely linked by blood and speech with the common people of England, and, moulded perhaps by the influences of feudalism, was still strikingly unchanged; that now it was the most distinctively national remnant on American soil, and symbolized the development of the continent, and that with it must go the last suggestions of the pioneers, with their hardy physiques, their speech, their manners and customs, their simple architecture and simple mode of life. It was soon plain to him, too, that a change was being wrought at last—the change of destruction. The older mountaineers, whose bewildered eyes watched the noisy signs of an unintelligible civilization, were passing away. Of the rest, some, sullen and restless, were selling their homesteads and following the spirit of their forefathers into a new wilderness; others, leaving their small farms in adjacent valleys to go to ruin, were gaping idly about the public works, caught up only too easily by the vicious current of the incoming tide. In a century the mountaineers must be swept away, and their ignorance of the tragic forces at work among them gave them an unconscious pathos that touched Clayton deeply.[5]

The novelette also records Fox's personal interest in his new subjects. Like Clayton, he went much among them; and, as he studied and wrote, he became more emotionally attached to the people he was to live among and to know better than most regional writers before him.

II *"A Cumberland Vendetta"*

It has been reported that, when Fox received a check for $262 from the Century Company for "A Mountain Europa," he was so pleased that he had the check photographed before cashing it and later had the picture displayed on the wall of his home at Big Stone Gap, Virginia.[6] The check or the publication also inspired the budding young author to attempt another story that he had started some time earlier: "A Cumberland Vendetta, a Tale of the Kentucky Mountains" (later described as a novel), published in the *Century* for June, July, and August, 1894. One year later it was the lead story in *A Cumberland Vendetta and Other Stories* (Harper's), and in 1899 and 1900 it was published by Harper's in a single-volume edition both in this country and in England.

That the story was any improvement on Fox's first mountain tale is doubtful. It concerns a topic he was to introduce in many a sketch that followed—the mountain feud. The Stetsons, Southern sympathizers during the Civil War, find their differences with the Union-supporting Lewallens exacerbated in the years that follow the struggle: "The war armed them, and brought back an ancestral contempt for human life; it left them a heritage of lawlessness that for mutual protection made necessary the very means used by their feudal forefathers; personal hatred supplanted its dead issues, and with them the war went on. . . . It was feudalism born again."[7]

The Stetson-Lewallen feud is interlaced with a love affair between a son and daughter of the opposing clans. The son, Rome Stetson, slow to anger and proud of his race, is driven at last to defend himself from the vendetta of the Lewallens; but his mission is complicated by his love for Martha Lewallen, daughter of old Jasper, the fiery head of the Lewallen family. A few shots are fired furtively from behind trees; eventually, the story reaches a climax with a pitched battle around the courthouse at Hazlan—"a little town five miles up the river, where Troubled Fork runs seething into the Cumberland."[8]

When Rome and his cohorts manage to surround some Lewallens caught in the courthouse, a siege ensues which is finally broken by Martha's riding in ostensibly to give her friends and relatives food but actually to provide guns and the means of their escape. The Stetson chivalry, evidenced by Rome's disavowal of "fightin' women," allows the escape; but the Lewallens have been decimated by the courthouse fight. When old Jasper dies as a result of his wounds, the feud dies down. Rome makes his way to the fatherless girl (she has long been motherless), and they decide to leave the mountains for a new home in the West.

Like Fox's earlier effort, "A Cumberland Vendetta" has thin character portrayal; the plot meanders, despite his attempts, on the advice of Richard Watson Gilder, to condense the story; but the descriptive passages are good. One reviewer noted that Fox had pictured landscape almost as if he had painted with brush and easel.[9] He could draw a scene, and he often does it well in this story. If he had been writing a personal essay or merely a sketch, he would have succeeded admirably. As a fictionist, he failed in a literary sense though the public scarcely recognized this failure.

"A Cumberland Vendetta" was inspired by events Fox had seen in Harlan County, Kentucky; and it is one of the few authentic sketches of Southern mountain feuding in American fiction. Too often this aspect of the mountaineer's history has been treated with high humor or burlesque, but Fox knew his nineteenth-century mountaineers and meant to depict them authentically. The obscure origins of the feud, the intensity of family pride, the flight to the West, the stubbornness of the older generation, and the attempts by a few in the younger group to break from the traditional pattern are amply recorded, as well as the peculiar code of the fighting itself.

This authentic phase of the story probably prompted the reviewer in *Bookman* to state his lack of sympathy with the class of people depicted in the tale: "Moonshine and pistols are the natural inspirations of every motive in life, and the accompaniments to every event and ceremony. A shock falls across the reader's mind to realize that such a community of lawlessness should exist in a country that calls itself civilized."[10] Laurence Hutton, who felt the same way in his *Harper's New Monthly Magazine* review, spoke of the "latent thirst for blood that must be underneath our civilization to appreciate such stories of feuding and violence."[11] Yet the public did appreciate them. "A Cumberland Vendetta" was undoubtedly effective in placing Fox more clearly before his readers as a delineator of mountain fiction at a time when quaintness and dialect were popular. The public wanted to know about the Kentucky mountains; Fox proposed to tell them.

III   *Other Sketches*

In quick succession, Fox fed the public appetite for local-color stories of the mountaineer. "The Last Stetson," a sequel to "A Cumberland Vendetta," appeared in *Harper's Weekly* for June 29, 1895. Chronicling the supposed sequence of events following the departure of Rome Stetson and Martha Lewallen of the earlier story from the mountains, Fox centers upon the boy Isom, half-brother to Rome, and the last of the Stetsons in the Hazlan region. A foundling, Isom has been left in the care of old Gabe Bunch, the miller. The boy's ways are queer—feeble-mindedness is suggested—and no one takes him very seriously. But, when the old Stetson-Lewallen feud appears to be on the verge of revival by hangers-on of both families, Isom brings a final peace to the warring parties. When Sherd Raines, the circuit rider of "A Mountain Europa," comes to Hazlan and works his powers to convert many of the mountain folk, Isom hears Sherd preach and is drawn to a "conviction," as the mountain folk call a conversion: "I've been skeered afore by riders a'tellin' 'bout the torments o' hell, but I never heerd nothin' like his tellin' 'bout the Lord," Isom avers.[12]

Prior to events in the story, Isom has killed young Jasper Lewallen when he was about to slay Rome by stealth. Affected by the thought of eternal damnation as the reward for killing as preached by Raines, Isom intervenes at a crucial moment in the renewed feud to warn Steve Brayton, a Lewallen ally, that Steve Marcum, Rome Stetson's old friend, is ready to ambush him. Isom's gesture, made at night when the ambush is to take place, is mistaken by the Braytons who fire at the boy and wound him. When it is discovered that Isom has come to the Brayton cabin "to save his life by losing it," all parties are so moved that Sherd Raines is able to effect new "convictions" and a permanent end to the feud.

About one fourth the length of "A Cumberland Vendetta," "The Last Stetson" is a vastly superior story. Old Gabe, the miller who has long sought to bring a halt to the killings, circuit rider Raines, and, above all, Isom Stetson are not only the best characters Fox had thus far portrayed but also among the best he was ever to do. Isom is suggestive of a type Fox later drew well—the young boy of early adolescence who struggles with the adult world and its code as he gropes for maturity. The dialect is remarkably clear and effective: phrases such as "Well, I hain't feelin' much peert" or "You'll ketch yer death o' cold swimmin' this way atter a fresh" reproduce with authentic tones the quaint speech of the Kentucky mountains. The story is less sentimental than many Fox did; all in all, it is a cleanly drawn vignette of a mountain boy and of mountain life.

Fox followed his success in "The Last Stetson" with a series of even shorter items for *Harper's Weekly* and the *Century* during 1895 and 1896. These stories—"Courtin' on Cutshin," "Through the Gap," "The Senator's Last Trade," "Grayson's Baby," "The Passing of Abraham Shivers," "Message in the Sand," and "Preachin' on Kingdom-Come"—continued the local-color regionalism and dialect patterns he had set for himself. Occasional stories or sketches of the bluegrass appeared in the magazines during the same time ("Fox-hunting in Kentucky" and "After Br'er Rabbit in the Bluegrass"), but mostly Fox was exploiting the literary treasures of the mountains.

In June, 1897, Harper and Brothers published a collection of these Kentucky mountaineer stories under the title of *Hell-fer-Sartain and Other Stories*. The volume proved to be one of Fox's better books and achieved an instant popularity with critics and public alike. In the *Hell-fer-Sartain* sketches Fox worked in the manner he knew best. In the ten short sketches, which deal exclusively with the mountain types, dialect is employed but is not overdone; the descriptive passages, as usual, are excellent; and, more important, the characters often come alive whereas in the longer works they do not. The book leaves the reader with the impression that Fox was better in the short story or the sketch than in the longer forms. Here he could employ the local color, the yarn-spinner tradition, the uniqueness of the Virginia and Kentucky mountaineer's way of life to better advantage.

"Grayson's Baby," which was drawn from an actual incident, records the warmth and sympathy of Grayson, the Virginian, for an infant child of a mountain woman who has been temporarily abandoned by her man and is unable to support her large family of children and step-children. The pride and suspicion of the mountain people are depicted in the woman's sullen acceptance of help and in her failure to display the gratitude obviously expected by her benefactors in the community.

"A Purple Rhododendron," the longest work in the collection, continues the story of Grayson. This time his love for a bluegrass belle is unrequited, or she falls in love with another (it is never quite clear which); and Grayson, who has earlier spoken of suicide during the business depression at the Gap, now tells the narrator of his determination to pluck the first purple rhododendron of the season for the girl. It is a suicidal mission, for the rhododendron blooms on a most inaccessible precipice of the mountain. But he makes good his promise—only to fall to his death in full view of the narrator, who sends the flower that Grayson has clutched to the young girl as a symbol of her broken pledge.

"Through the Gap" is a slight account of a mountain couple who come over the Gap from Kentucky into southwestern Virginia, ostensibly to be married. But the mountaineer turns to playing with fast women, and the mountain girl goes off with a "half-breed Malungian." Later the girl returns, the two lovers are reconciled and married, and they return through the Gap to their Cumberland home. The story is noteworthy for Fox's introduction of the Malungian character, a man drawn from an actual group of isolated people, supposedly of mixed nationality and racial strains, found only in upper East Tennessee and southwestern Virginia.

Several of the best sketches of the collection are told in native dialect by a shrewd mountaineer narrator. "On Hell-fer-Sartain Creek," for example, is one of the best stories Fox ever wrote and the first one to bring him widespread national attention.[13] Only three pages long, it is a masterful condensation of the droll humor and tragicomic situation that the mountain life so often illustrated; and the atmosphere and the tone are nearly perfect. Two mountain wooers, Rich Harp and Harve Hall, are lured into a fight over the girl Nance Osborn. The fight, it develops, has been engineered by a third party, Abe Shivers, who makes off with the girl while the two men recuperate from their blows. Discovering the trick by which they have been victimized, Harve and Rich draw straws to see which one will get revenge. The story ends in cryptic fashion. Another dancing party is planned for Christmas night; but, we are assured, Abe won't be there: "He's a'settin' by a bigger fire, I reckon (ef he ain't in it), a-bitin' his thumbs."[14] Whether Fox drew the incident from life or not (there is a Hell-fer-Sartain Creek in Leslie and Perry counties, Kentucky), the sketch seems accurate enough of the slow, droll, matter-of-fact way of mountain justice.

"The Passing of Abraham Shivers" and "A Trick O' Trade" also portray the many sly tricks, practical jokes, and acts of downright meanness of one of Fox's best drawn minor characters. The narrator of the first story remarks that Abe has done considerable good "jes by dyin'." His sins are so manifold that the Creator will have a time-consuming task reckoning up the account: "An' ef thar's only one Jedgment Day, the Lawd'll nuver git to us."[15] "A Trick O' Trade" is in the old southwestern yarn-spinner tradition, with Abe Shivers again as the protagonist; but he is bested this time in a scheme of devilment by "old Tom Perkins."

At least three of the stories provide unusually penetrating insights into the Kentucky mountain life of the author's time. "Courtin' on Cutshin" delightfully presents the quaint courtship customs of the people. "Settin' up with a gal" and "talkin' to her" are illustrated in the story of a reluctant lover and his girl. "The Message in the Sand" makes use of a biblical allusion in recording the spirit with which the mountaineers forgive the fallen woman, while turning their wrath on the man guilty of the seduction. "Whut you reckon the Lawd kep' a'writin' thar on the groun' that day when them fellers was a-pesterin' him about that pore woman? ... I tell ye, brother, he writ thar jes what I'm al'ays a-sayin'. Hit hain't the woman's fault."[16] "The Senator's Last Trade," based on a political figure that Fox knew in the mountains, shows the trading capacities of the shrewd native bargainer and the pathos in the passing of a man who has known better days.

"Preachin' on Kingdom Come," one of the best of the sketches, is another portrait of Sherd Raines, the circuit rider. The narrator tells how Raines brought peace to the Day-Dillon feud on Kingdom-Come Creek with his powerful preaching. The entire sketch is recorded in a dialect that is amply illustrated in the following account of the preacher's sermon:

Stranger, that long preacher talked jes as easy as I'm a-talkin' now, an' hit was p'int-blank as the feller from Hazlan said. You jes ought 'a' heerd him tellin' about the Lawd a'bein' as pore as any feller thar, an' a-makin' barns an' fences an' ox-yokes an' sech like; an' not a-bein' able to write his own name—havin' to make his mark mebbe—when he started out to save the world. An' how they tuk him an' nailed him onto a cross when he'd come down fer nothin' but to save 'em; an' stuck a spear big as a corn-knife into his side, an' give him vinegar; an' his own mammy a-standin' down thar on the ground a-cryin' an' a-watchin' him; an' he a-fergivin' all of 'em then an' thar![17]

Although George Merriam Hyde questioned in *Bookman* the current rage for dialect stories, he found Fox had not exaggerated the usage in his *Hell-fer-Sartain* collection. Hyde was impressed with the strong sense of reality beneath the rough exterior of the tales: "His mountaineers have something elemental in them which makes them interesting despite their strangeness."[18] A reviewer for *Critic*, who also was favorably impressed with the sketches, complimented Fox on his ability at condensations: "With a single exception, none of his sketches is more than a few pages long, and yet each leaves on the mind . . . the distinct impression of a clean cut etching, and is richly impregnated with human interest." The reviewer correctly noted that the sketches were probably written for public readings and that, to get their true impact, they should be read aloud.[19] Laurence Hutton in *Harper's New Monthly Magazine* commented on Fox's gift at storytelling, while the *Nation* reviewer was impressed with Fox's picturing of the life in the Cumberlands: "In accurate reproduction of dialect and custom, in swift and successful characterization, they leave little to be desired."[20]

When Charles E. L. Wingate wrote an article on Fox for *Critic* magazine in July, 1897, he prophesied great popularity for the author because "he writes interestingly; he paints with words powerfully; he has opened a new field."[21] *Hell-fer-Sartain* proved Wingate correct. From 1897 on Fox was well known to the reading public, and he increasingly received the attention of critics. No longer provincial in his appeal, he had a nation-wide audience that assured him a steady, profitable career in literature.

CHAPTER 3

Mountain and Bluegrass Contrasts

I *Boom and Bust at the Gap*

A S THE BOOM in the Cumberland Mountain coal and iron regions burgeoned, the Fox brothers moved their base of operations from Jellico, Tennessee, to Big Stone Gap, Virginia, about sixty miles northeast of the more celebrated Cumberland Gap. The Gap, as the little Virginia town was often called, had suddenly come to life in the early 1890's because it was thought to be well situated for taking advantage of the nearby mineral deposits; on a high plateau between two streams that converged to make the Powell River, it was obviously located at a natural gap through the Cumberlands from Virginia into Kentucky. And it was near coal deposits to the north and iron to the south; furthermore, there was limestone in between for the processing of the iron into steel. Because great things were expected of this area by 1890, speculators and entrepreneurs entered the region to exploit the mineral deposits; hotels were built to accommodate the expected influx of residents; railroads were rapidly penetrating the area. It was believed that the Gap would become the center of an outstanding industrial community that might someday rival Pittsburgh.

In 1890, John William Fox, Sr., moved with his family from the bluegrass area of Kentucky to Big Stone Gap, Virginia, where three of his sons, James, Horace, and John, Jr., were becoming local Napoleons of finance and development. During many months of the early 1890's, John Fox, Jr., worked in partnership with his brother James to buy land and develop the mineral resources of the Gap region. Fox had made contacts with wealthy people several years earlier, first at Harvard and later in New York as a newspaperman. As he continued his career in writing, he met other wealthy patrons of the arts and artists. There were

[37]

also well-to-do friends in Louisville and Lexington. Some of these acquaintances helped the Fox brothers with loans and independent investments during these years. The novelist spent more time, indeed, during the early years of the decade managing his land interests and developments in Big Stone Gap and traveling in the furtherance of these developments than he did in literary endeavors.

But the panic of 1893 came, and the economic bonanza at the Gap suddenly collapsed. Eastern and English capital that had flowed into the general area of Cumberland Gap suddenly was withdrawn; capitalists were no longer able to extend their credit for investments in the Southern mountains. Land values dropped, building came to a halt, the railroad's thrust was temporarily blunted, and it was soon apparent that Big Stone Gap would have to wait a while to become "the Pittsburgh of the South." Instead of getting rich, almost everybody, including the Fox brothers, was left broke and in debt.

Some bluegrass Kentuckians who had migrated to the mountains to profit from the expected good times went home chastened by their experience, but the Foxes stayed on. The father, who had retired from teaching, felt no sense of urgency to leave the mountain scenery he had quickly come to admire. Actually, he never returned to Kentucky permanently, but lived out his days in the home the family had built at the Gap. James and Horace Fox persisted for a time in their faith in the possibilities of the town: the coal wealth was there and would eventually be mined. James finally did achieve considerable success in real estate and mining, years later moving the base of his operations to New York and expanding to overseas connections.

John, Jr., meanwhile, found new time on his hands to turn to his primary interest—the writing of the many mountain stories earlier described. His trips back into the hills of Kentucky in connection with the Fox land and mining ventures—particularly into Letcher, Leslie, Harlan, and Perry counties—and his experiences in pioneering the Gap had provided him with the subjects he was soon exploring in his fictional sketches. The collapse of 1893, therefore, turned out to be a stroke of good fortune for him. Though he was to know difficult times in the immediate years ahead (life for a while seemed to be a constant struggle to get out of debt), he soon discovered that the surest way to success was with the pen; and he was never to consider any other endeavor from that point on.

II   *Public Reading and Lecturing*

At the same time, to help meet his financial needs, Fox had adopted a peripheral career suggested to him by a beloved and lifelong friend, Thomas Nelson Page—reading and lecturing on the public platform.[1] Fox had displayed a talent for oratory as far back as his Kentucky University days. Later at Harvard his interest in the theater was pronounced. At one time, as noted earlier, he had halfheartedly thought of a career on the stage. Then in the 1890's, searching for new means of financial betterment, he decided to give public readings from his works: his exploitation of the mountain dialect in fiction could be implemented by public readings of dialect stories. Fox, who always had a keen ear for the patterns of mountain speech, could reproduce it orally with realistic perfection. In writing a recommendation for him for the Southern Lyceum Bureau, Thomas Nelson Page said in 1894:

He has a clear musical voice of great sweetness as well as carrying power, if he will use it as I have heard him use it; he understands the dialect of the mountains of Virginia and Kentucky as few people in this country do, and he is perfectly natural. If you want elocution, he is not the man, but let him and his friends thank heaven for it. I feel sure that if you will open the way for Mr. Fox to appear before some of the audiences which you know so well, he will prove one of the most popular readers you could find in this country, and you could not get anything better to read in public than scenes from his own stories.[2]

Page's prophecy proved accurate; Fox's fame as a reader of mountain dialect stories spread rapidly, and he was soon in great demand at a time when platform reading was one of the most popular forms of public entertainment. Always, his rendering of the mountain dialect impressed audiences; it was simple and unaffected; he never indulged in the histrionic; he did not elocute. But the true ring of mountain speech was in his delivery and manner and he never failed to communicate it to his listeners. Many of his first mountain sketches were written as vehicles for this reading, so there was his own distinctive style in almost everything he read. For the most part, his programs consisted of his own material which he knew thoroughly. Later he went under the management of Major J. B. Pond, and his fame as a reader was assured. He appeared before colleges and literary clubs throughout the East and South. Periodically, he left his home base at Big Stone Gap to engage in these reading and lecture tours. He combined forces with James Whitcomb Riley on two occasions, Riley becoming one of his close friends; and he also appeared with Bill Nye and George Washington Cable at various times.

Perhaps Fox's success as a reader was demonstrated best, however, through the invitations he received several years later from an old friend in the White House. Fox had met Theodore Roosevelt in 1894, shortly after the future President had written the young author expressing his admiration of "A Cumberland Vendetta." Over the years, Roosevelt was to continue his enthusiasm for Fox's writings; and after he became President, he invited Fox to the White House to give a reading of dialect stories. Fox augmented his performance with mountain songs sung to the accompaniment of his own guitar playing. Here again he seems to have been eminently successful, for he was invited back several times to entertain Roosevelt's guests.

III The Kentuckians

Meanwhile, as Fox turned to reading his mountain works from the stage, he began to exploit in fiction his native bluegrass region of Kentucky. *The Kentuckians,* his first novel, appeared serially in *Harper's* from July through October, 1897, and was published as a book in December of the same year. It was a departure from Fox's earlier writing. Though a mountaineer and mountain ways play an important part in the novel, the book's primary setting is in the bluegrass; and the purpose is not primarily to reveal mountain mores but to contrast the two centers of life in the state—the cultured, civilized bluegrass and the uncultured, rough mountain counties of the East.

John Fox was himself, of course, a product of both areas. Though he was born in the bluegrass and nurtured on the traditions of that prideful region, he loved the mountains and remembered that his own forebears had crossed them to get to the Kentucky heartland. He saw the virtues and the vices of both sections, and it became increasingly his self-imposed assignment to interpret each to each and both to the world. *The Kentuckians* was his first venture with this objective.

The novel basically concerns two men and a woman. Randolph Marshall is born to the purple, a son of bluegrass parentage and inheritor of all that status and tobacco plantation culture might bring; Boone Stallard, on the other hand, is a mountain man—schooled at Transylvania, but largely unsophisticated and possessing a great native intelligence and keen drive to make something better of himself than his mountain environment promises. The young woman in the story, Anne Bruce, is the daughter of the governor of the state and a flowering beauty of Kentucky bluegrass womanhood. Unofficially pledged to Marshall in matrimony, Anne is drawn to Stallard when she meets him in the state capital.

In the two principal male characters, Fox draws his contrasting image of the state's two major regions. And in the state capital of Frankfort he brings the two men together as they serve in the state legislature. "These men of the mountains and the people of the blue-grass are the extremes of civilization in the State," he wrote.[3] The bluegrass represents old-fashioned grace and dignity, traditions, manners, and gallantry. The mountains, on the other hand, are the scene of feuds, ambuscades, treachery, narrow parochialism, ignorance, and, above all, lawlessness.

But Fox goes to great lengths to show that both strains derived from the same source. Originally, all the Kentucky settlers came over the mountains from ،irginia. The majority of the migrants, who went on through the mountain passes to the bluegrass and regions to the west where the geography and climate were hospitable, took their place in the forward march of the nation. Some of the migrants, however, remained along the way in the mountain fastnesses where they became isolated because of the hostile geography; and the world passed them by.

The mountain people were not to be blamed for the backwardness that resulted from their isolation: "They had lived apart from the world and without books, schools, or churches since the Revolution; they had had a century of such a life in which to deteriorate. Their law was lax. They lived apart from one another as well, and, of necessity, public sentiment was weak and unity of action difficult—except for mischief."[4] But there were also good men in the mountains: "The good ninety were there for every ten that were bad."[5]   Unfortunately, however, the bad men gave the area its reputation. But any people left outside the mainstream of civilization, as the mountain people had been, would have remained in their primitive state or failed to advance. The powerful environment had made them what they were; they could advance into the light of the modern world only by their own strength and their own virtues which were not meager after all.

Randolph Marshall, famed orator of the state legislature, has proposed a measure to disband Roland County.[6] He feels that the disgrace of the lawless atmosphere created there by the Keaton-Stallard feud is too much for the state to bear. In a scathing speech, he castigates the mountain people for their backwardness and ignorance; and he seemingly suggests they are more than a small stain on the state's reputation. Boone Stallard, serving in the legislature for his native county of Roland, responds. He, too, is an orator of no mean talents. (Fox was writing at a time when oratory was still honored in the Southern tradition.) The clash between the two men is inevitable.

Meanwhile, the governor's daughter, Anne Bruce, has met Stallard and has been drawn by his strange power and magnetism. She senses a man of great natural talent handicapped by his mean birth and mountain inheritance. On the other hand, her sweetheart of early days, Marshall, who has the advantage of fine background, has failed to achieve the goals he should have set for himself. Among other things, Marshall has at times been given to flippancy and to alcoholism, and he is inclined to be petulant and to indulge in rages, particularly when prompted by romantic jealousies. As Anne knows Stallard better, she likes Marshall less.

But there is a shadow in Stallard's life. His brother is in the state penitentiary in Frankfort because of a murder he has committed in the feuding of Roland County. This brother, who is of a much lower caliber than Boone, is a source of great embarrassment to the young legislator as he attempts to bring law and order to his region. The brother also stands as a symbolic reminder to Boone of the inability to bridge the two worlds of his inheritance and his dreams.

While Stallard is serving in Frankfort, the Keaton-Stallard feud erupts at home. When Stallard appeals to the governor for troops, the governor is powerless to send them. (Just why is never explained.) Stallard determines to go back to Roland

County himself to force the issue. For years he has been able to keep himself above the actual fighting. He has argued for law and peaceful order. Indeed, following his graduation from the university where he had gone to study for the ministry but had turned to the law instead, he had returned to the mountains to argue the case for legal justice and redress. But the new feud promises to undo all he has accomplished. In a pitched gun battle that follows the latest outbreak, Stallard achieves the order he desires for the community, rallies the good people of the county to his cause, and restores peace and law to the area. But he gives up his legislative seat to remain where he is most needed—at home.

He returns to the state capital once more to explain his new position to Anne. Quite by accident she and Marshall learn of his brother in the penitentiary. In what seems like an act of sympathy, she offers to go with Stallard to the mountains. But Stallard feels that she is moved at this crisis only by a sense of pity. So he refuses her help.

The novel ends abruptly, leaving the love story unresolved. E. F. Harkins complained later that many people were bothered by the ambiguity of the ending.[7] Fox does not say directly whether Anne married Stallard or Marshall. A close reading of the text would indicate that she finally chose Marshall, however. It was best that she did, for it would be difficult to imagine the polished Anne Bruce having much in common with Stallard's pipe-smoking mother and his barefooted sister of the mountain cabin. At least, Fox makes so much of this contrast that it would have been an incongruous match. Indeed, all through the novel Anne wonders that she can be so attracted to Stallard, given his uncouth background and the feuding tradition of his kin; and Stallard is so stung by the contrasting ways of the two cultures that his anticipated proposal to Anne is never made. As a result, the novel is marred by an incredulity that is matched only by its sentimentality.

But the book is less a love story than a delineation of the contrasting types in Kentucky's history. The *Critic,* which noted this quality in its review of the novel, added: "It is difficult to decide whether the matter or the manner of this book deserves the greater praise. . . . This tale of strong men assumes an importance that places it beyond the ranks of local tales to which it might be thought to belong, and makes it part of the greater literature that is of the world."[8] The point Fox was making was that all Kentuckians—all men, perhaps—are, at heart, as one: mountaineer yeoman and bluegrass colonel have fine qualities. Marshall recognizes this fact in the story; and, in truth, the example of Stallard spurs him to realize his own potential, to cease his reliance on his sentimental attachment to Anne, and to be independent for the first time. Late in the story Marshall also recognizes Stallard's greatness despite the mountaineer's handicaps. As for Stallard, he knows full well the advantages and worth of culture and civilization; he had been attracted by the ideal of Anne Bruce. If he could not quite gain the political goal in life that he might once have sought, he could still appreciate the qualities of life represented by the bluegrass group.

The novel has the best character portrayal Fox had yet created. Boone Stallard, who contrasts vividly with the stereotyped Marshall and with the insipid Anne, stands in the forefront of all of Fox's characters. Fox said he had been modeled after an actual mountain figure named Boone Logan. It was a happy choice. He seems just strong enough for Fox's purpose and yet is not overdrawn: he is not inordinately good, not too much the polished provincial. He is painted to show the mountaineer's qualities at their best—his potential if given opportunity—and not to illustrate his backwardness or savagery. Stallard is convincing and informative at the same time.

Because of Stallard, the book is more successful as a character study than as a plot. That Fox probably intended this imbalance is indicated by a letter he wrote Charles Wingate in August, 1897. Wingate had inquired about the possibilities of doing a drama version of *The Kentuckians*. Fox doubted that the book could be turned into a play. "It is," he wrote, "a story of character, not of incident, and, in a sense, it is a rather daring experiment. I deliberately suppress dramatic possibilities in the story— and I lead the reader to a spiritual conflict in Marshall—at home —when the reader is looking for a howling fight in the mountains. Finally, the full characterization of Marshall is left to the last chapter, almost the last page. This is subverting the laws of development and construction in one way and I'm curious about the result."[9] But it is not Marshall who commands the reader's interest; it is the sturdy mountaineer who dominates the novel's pages.

William Morton Payne noted that *The Kentuckians* was "the

most serious piece of work thus far attempted by this growing writer."[10] He stated that Fox did not sermonize overmuch, but he explained the mountaineer's condition more ably perhaps than a purely local-color story writer might have done. The *Critic* and some other journals had now placed Fox in the company of Bret Harte, Sarah Orne Jewett, and Mary Wilkins Freeman.[11] But *The Kentuckians* is not in the Mary Noailles Murfree tradition: there is little dialect and only a little incidental lore. The book is, first, an explanation to the sophisticated outsider of the mountaineer's backwardness and, second, a study in contrasts of bluegrass and mountain types. Of the latter, Fox was to write much more in the future.

CHAPTER 4

The Spanish-American War

I   *War Reporting*

JOHN FOX filled two outstanding roles as a correspondent after his experiences on the New York *Sun* and the New York *Times*. In 1898, he went to Cuba as a correspondent for *Harper's Weekly*; and, in 1904, he went as a *Scribner's* correspondent to the Orient to report the Russo-Japanese War.[1] Of the two experiences, the Spanish-American War proved more valuable in terms of Fox's later writing. Not only did he send home some good reporting for *Harper's,* but he also gained information and story material he was to use in a later novel.

Fox had grown somewhat dissatisfied with the publishing house of Harper and Brothers by the spring of 1898. The firm had expressed a willingness to take any materials he might write but would make no commitment about the financial remuneration it was willing to extend. Annoyed by such equivocation, he was in a minor huff with the publishing house when the Spanish-American War broke out. Nevertheless, the editor of *Harper's* wired him in April, 1898, to see if he would be willing to go to Chickamauga, New Orleans, and Tampa to report activities in the training camps. Later he was assigned to Cuba to report the war action overseas.

Fox accepted the appointment with alacrity not only for the financial return it might bring but also because of his enthusiasm for the war effort. He was not among those writers who opposed either the war in Cuba or its aftermath; instead, he gave almost jingoistic support to the flag wherever it went. He immediately wired his friend Theodore Roosevelt to see about the possibility of serving with the Rough Riders. Roosevelt eventually arranged a place for him with his volunteer cavalry regiment, and Fox did cover some of the Rough Riders' activities in Cuba. But, for the most part, he was with General Shafter's divisions at Santiago. Meanwhile, in April, May, and June, 1898, he had the more monotonous assignment of reporting activities in the training camps in the United States.

He went first to Chickamauga Park outside Chattanooga, one of the assembly and training points for both regular and volunteer army groups. When he wrote his impressions in *Harper's Weekly* in May and June, 1898, the whole war effort seemed to him, as it did to many citizens that spring, more like a lark than a serious endeavor. He told of how the civilians came to see the color and excitement of an army camp:

Sunday was a vast local holiday for a swarm of curious civilians to the same spot; for hundreds of miles around: on train, farm-wagon, spring-wagon, buggy, horseback, foot; on bicycle, in open landau, carriage, cart; in express-wagons, baggage-wagons, omnibuses; in barges with projecting additions and other land craft beyond classification or description. And the people! Rich whites, whites well-to-do, and poor white trash; good country folks, valley-farmers, farmers from spurs and table-lands; subjects from the "Kingdom of Dude"; Craddock's mountaineers and Harris's crackers; darkies; and the motley feminine horde that the soldier draws the world over—all moving along a road between Lookout on the right and Missionary Ridge on the left, and interspersed here and there with a clanking troop of horse or a rumbling battery—all anxious to look upon these long-neglected war-children who seem now in a fair way to come to their own at last.[2]

He was impressed, as a Southerner of his time might have been, with the Negro troops—a novel sight for a Kentuckian—and wondered if they would fight, only to be assured that they would; in fact, the trouble might be to curb them once they got started, their officers reported. Although Fox's questioning of Negro troops revealed his Southern prejudices, he later tried to be fair in recording their qualities.

When he visited Atlanta and Confederate General Gordon, who seemed to symbolize something the war was doing—drawing North and South permanently together again, Fox quoted Gordon as saying "there are no sectional or state lines now, when a common enemy is to be met."[3] He described Camp Northen at Griffin, Georgia, and the arrival of the first Spanish prisoners at Fort McPherson in Atlanta. Finally, he went back to the bluegrass and reported the gathering of volunteers on the lawn of Ashland, home of Henry Clay, at Lexington: "It was like a picnic-ground. All the soldiers who were not on actual duty seemed to go where they pleased and do what they pleased, and they were flirting and playing pranks and singing like a crowd of undergraduates on a lark."[4] He reported that one group of mountaineer volunteers contained men so tall they were rejected for military service. He also noted that the Kentucky men were following in the path of the "gallant Crittenden" who in 1851 had fought another fight in Cuba and was martyred along with one hundred fifty other Kentuckians. The mention of Colonel William L. Crittenden suggested the use Fox was to make of these materials in a future novel.

In June, Fox finally got to Tampa where he waited on the docks and then on shipboard in the bay for the Cuba sailing. Finally, he departed, attached to Shafter's Army as a *Harper's* correspondent. On June 19, he wrote his family, "I can't get over the idea that it is simply a big picnic."[5] "No danger whatever," he wrote later from the Hill of Las Guasimas.[6] His dispatches, entitled "With the Troops for Santiago," appeared in the *Harper's Weekly* for July 16, 1898. The first entry, written from Tampa on June 12, told of the waiting, and castigated those who had not prepared for this war: "The trouble is with the men and the people who have blindly refused to recognize the possibility of the emergency now upon us—the land-lubber of the Western interior, the rural Populists, and the city agitators, and the tender hearts of Boston."[7]

The next entry on June 20 was written at sea near Santiago: "In spite of transport and war-ship, officer and soldier, I cannot realize that this is war; that this is not some strange huge excursion; that we are not to land in peace and safety, and in peace and safety go back as we came; that even at this moment a little farther down these gashed mountains, showing ever clearer through the mist, are enemies with whom the officers and soldiers around me may soon be in a death-grapple."[8] Fox praised the common soldier who seemed to endure so much with so little complaining. The third entry (June 22) described a landing of Lawton's and Chaffee's men of Shafter's army at Baiquiri near Santiago and the taking of a Spanish blockhouse on a small nearby hill. The Spanish fled; there were no casualties. The account could have been mock-heroic, but Fox seriously wrote of it.

In an article for July 30, 1898, Fox described the "first battle on Cuban soil," Las Guasimas, a skirmish in which the First United States Cavalry and some five hundred of the Rough Riders were involved. He noted the criticism that had been leveled at the Rough Riders in particular because of this engagement. They had overextended themselves in their eagerness and had fallen into a minor ambush: "But, all granted, for the sake of argument, what then? Who remembers a military mistake when there is a deathless ideal of courage under it? I imagine the Riders would prefer a reprimand for being too far in front to one for being too far behind. . . . The fight was a perfect exhibition of dauntless courage. So let critical lips be dumb, let Old Glory and the flag of the one star wave together, and wave long and high. And from American and Cuban, to regular and Rider, with one throat—and for the Rider let it be opened wide—Hail!"[9]

"Santiago and Caney" and "Truce" reported the fighting at Santiago. On July 23, July 30, and August 6 his dispatches about the Santiago front appeared; they had been written during and right after the battle of July 1 and 2, 1898. In "Santiago and Caney" he wrote some of his most realistic prose and sounded more like fellow correspondent Stephen Crane rather than his own admirer, Richard Harding Davis. The work is generally devoid of the sentiment that mars so much of his fiction. In describing the wounded of that battle he wrote:

At this point began the central lane of death, and the terrible procession to the rear was on its way. Men with arms in slings; men with trousers torn away at the knee and bandaged legs; men with brow, face, mouth, or throat swathed; men with no shirts, but a broad swathe around the chest or stomach—each bandage grotesquely pictured with human figures printed to show how it should be bound on whatever part of the body the bullet entered. Men staggering along unaided, or between two comrades, or borne on litters, some white and quiet, some groaning and blood-stained, some conscious, some dying, some using a rifle for support, or a stick thrust through the side of a tomato-can, and not a crutch to be seen. Rolls, haversacks, blouses, hard-tack, Bibles, strewn by the way-side where the soldiers had thrown them before they went into action. Nearly all of the wounded were dazed and drunken in appearance, except at the brows, which were tightly drawn with pain. One man with short, thick, up-right red hair, stumbling from one side of the road to the other, with no wound apparent, and muttering: "Oh, I don't know what happened to me. I don't know what happened to me."

Another, hopping across the creek on one leg—the other bare and wounded—and using his gun, muzzle down, as a vaulting-pole. Another, with his arm in the sling, pointing out the way to me.

"Take this road," he said. "I don't know where that one goes, but I know this one. I went up this one and I brought back a souvenir," he added, cheerily.

Another tall handsome fellow, a Rough Rider, whom I remembered having seen at social functions in Washington last winter, whom I next saw at Tampa standing for an hour in the hot sun with his roll, and whom I saw now with his hand bandaged—weak, white, trembling, but walking alone, still gentle, considerate, uncomplaining, asserting that he was not hurt except in his hand, and not mentioning the bullet in his chest. I saw him again next morning a mile further down the road, after he had slept in the woods all night with his wound undressed, much weaker, more feverish, but still saying he needed no help, still anxious to give nobody the slightest trouble; and next day I saw him sitting in the hot sun at Siboney, ten miles further on (he had walked the whole way, I think), waiting to get to a hospital-ship—and confessing, at last, that he would like to have a canned peach. He had been shot lying down, and the bullet went through his hat, scraped through the skin along his temple, passed through the palm of his hand, and lodged in his chest. . . . I hope he will pull through, and I'd like him to know that I got his canned peach, with a doctor's order, but that he was on his way to the ship when I got back to his hot resting-place in the sand. Such a man and such a spirit has not been hard to find in this fight.[10]

In "Truce," published August 13 in *Harper's*, he told of the end of the Battle of Santiago. He had unkind things to say for the commanding officer, General Shafter. While the United States flag was going up in Santiago and the American troops were drawn up in ceremony outside the city, "the commanding officer was suffering himself to be involved in a street squabble, and demeaning himself, his flag, the people whom he served, and the soldiers whose worship he should have earned."[11] Fox spoke of the officer's dislike of correspondents and the "rasping oaths" that formed the chief part of the general's vocabulary. Later, it was said that Fox and Frederic Remington, the illustrator and a fellow correspondent, disliked General Shafter because he had not given them special privileges.[12] Shafter was soon to be involved in charges of failure to provide adequate medical and other supplies for his troops, and Fox might have been drawn into more controversy had he not fallen ill with fever during the campaign. He gave up his correspondent's assignment to return home right after the surrender. "Truce" was his last dispatch from the Cuban front.

II *The War Novel:* Crittenden

Harper's paid Fox $564 for his war correspondence and for subsequent use of the dispatches in *Harper's Pictorial History of the War with Spain.* Fox had gone to Cuba partly to gather data for a novel, however, and the literary rewards of the venture were more significant than any financial return he derived. In a letter to Charles Wingate written in January, 1898, Fox had expressed the seriousness with which he was now pursuing his literary career: "You see, I have written devilish little, and have never regarded my work seriously until lately. In fact, I'm still an amateur and with ill health, business and bad eyes (I can't use them yet at night) I haven't really honestly got down to work until this year. So that I feel and hope that I'm just beginning."[13] The Spanish-American War had been a useful interlude for a writer, but the typhoid fever that he brought out of Cuba kept him from renewing his writing activities until 1899. By then, he was eager to get back to work.

After recuperating at home, with friends in Maine, and briefly with Theodore Roosevelt at Sagamore Hill during the fall of 1898 and the winter of 1899, Fox began his next writing. He refused the offer of an assignment to the Hawaiian Islands for *Harper's* and turned instead for a publishing outlet to Charles Scribner's Sons, the firm that was to publish his work for the rest of his life. His first publications for *Scribner's Magazine* appeared in June and September, 1900. "Down the Kentucky on a Raft" and "To the Breaks of Sandy" were distilled from personal experiences in the Kentucky mountains and in the Gap area earlier in the 1890's. Subsequently, they were included in the volume *Blue-grass and Rhododendron* and belong more properly to a discussion of that work.

His Spanish-American War novel, *Crittenden: A Kentucky Story of Love and War,* was Fox's first major contribution under the Scribner's imprint. Over a year in the making, the novel was first published in November, 1900; Constable and Company issued a London edition in March, 1905. The book was dedicated to Joseph Stickney, "the master of Ballyhoo," and one of Fox's

wealthy Eastern friends. Ballyhoo was Stickney's country estate
on the Hudson River where Fox had often visited and where he
partially recovered from the fever contracted during the war.
Many sections of *Crittenden* came directly from Fox's Spanish-
American War dispatches—a few were even transplanted word
for word. The incidents and descriptions so nearly parallel Fox's
own experiences of 1898 that the war reporting seems only a
prelude for this larger effort.

The novel is concerned with Clay Crittenden, a descendant
of John Crittenden, pre-Civil War filibusterer in Cuba. Crittenden is a bluegrass Bourbon whose ancestors came over the Wilderness Road to forge a new land in Kentucky. His heritage is
a great one—state leaders in all branches of his family. But,
somehow, he has never quite realized his own potential in life.
Like Marshall in *The Kentuckians,* Crittenden has been disappointed in love and has led a life of periodic dissipation to
assuage his wounded feelings. Sometime before the story opens,
Judith Page has apparently jilted him for another; and Crittenden has fled to the mountains to ease his disappointment.

The story begins as he returns to the bluegrass at the precise
time that word has come of the war with Spain. Here, surely, is
an opportunity to forget his emotional sufferings and perhaps to
make something of himself in the nation's cause. So he volunteers to fight—largely, we are told, because he could do nothing
else. "There had been a Crittenden in every war of the nation—
down to the two Crittendens who slept side by side in the old
graveyard below the garden. And the Crittenden—of whom he
had spoken that morning—the gallant Crittenden who led his
Kentuckians to death in Cuba, in 1851, was his father's elder
brother."[14]

After a maudlin departure scene with his mother and a furtive
backward glance at Judith Page, whom he still loves, he goes to
camp at Chickamauga. For the camp scenes Fox drew on those
he had observed in April, 1898, while writing as a correspondent
for *Harper's;* in fact, the Chickamauga descriptions are based
directly on his reportorial dispatches. Crittenden, like Fox, views
the scene more as the depiction of a gay holiday than as a serious
war effort. He is impressed with the dedication of a Confederate
monument on Chickamauga battlefield, and he looks in wonder
at the Negro troops in camp. Earlier, he had thought, "The mere
idea of negro soldiers was not only repugnant to him, but he

did not believe in negro regiments."¹⁵ He had fancied that bringing Negroes into the services might hasten a race war in the South. Gradually, however, he adjusts to the idea of the Negro troops—though clearly considering them a novelty.

Finally, · Crittenden entrains for Tampa where he waits interminably for the trip to Cuba. Eventually departure comes, and once again he is impressed by the lightness of the whole affair: "It was a tropical holiday—that sail down to Cuba—a strange, huge pleasure-trip of steamships, sailing in a lordly column of three. . . . Music night and morning, on each ship, and music coming across the little waves at any hour from the ships about. . . . But nobody was looking for a fight—nobody thought the Spaniard would fight—and so these were only symbols of war; and even they seemed merely playing the game."¹⁶

Once in Cuba, he is thrown into the Santiago struggle where he meets the Rough Riders with whom his brother Basil serves. Fox stresses the value of the Rough Riders as symbolic of national unity: "Every state in the Union had a son in its ranks, and the sons represented every social element in the national life. Never was there a more representative body of men, nor a body of more varied elements standing all on one and the same basis of American manhood."¹⁷ There are also complimentary references to Roosevelt who, it is suggested, is already on his way to the White House.

Crittenden fights through the El Caney struggle before Santiago, is wounded, lies unattended at Siboney, contracts malarial fever, and is finally hospitalized. After such harrowing experiences, he returns home soon after the war ends in August. His recovery is abetted when he learns that Judith Page has experienced only a momentary infatuation with her erstwhile lover, her cousin Jack Page, and has really been in love with him all along. Jack Page, volunteering for military service under the name of Blackford, is a brave gallant who cannot control a yen for gambling and brawling. Consequently, he is cashiered from the Regular Army several months before the war with Spain begins; but he appears with the Rough Riders in Cuba and fights valiantly in some of the same skirmishes with Clay Crittenden. Crittenden, who knows him only as Blackford, comes to admire him greatly, and is present when Blackford is killed in Cuba. Only at the end of the story does Crittenden learn that Blackford is really Jack Page, Judith's earlier love. The novel ends with Crittenden's marriage to Judith (on the same day that his brother marries his betrothed) and with the reiterated statement that "God was good that Christmas."

As a love story, *Crittenden* is a complete failure. Fox was seldom very convincing in love scenes, but this book has the worst in all his fiction. No more sentimental rubbish exists than some of the passages in which Crittenden wrestles with his conscience or where he attempts to communicate his true feelings to Judith. No doubt such scenes moved the audiences of the genteel *fin de siècle,* but today's reader wonders that the two people could have failed to understand each other and could have muddled through a romantic situation as they did. The ending is almost grotesquely melodramatic.

Although Fox attempted a love story in *Crittenden,* he also intended to preach national unity. He viewed the Spanish-American War as a cementing bond that would bring North and South together again and create one nation. Clay Crittenden's own family had been symbolic of the Civil War division—his father had fought with the Confederacy; his father's brother, with the Union. By the end of the Spanish-American War, Crittenden feels he is more American than Southern. As he views the flag, a strange new feeling surges through him: "For then and there, Crittenden, Southerner, died straightway and through a travail of wounds, suffering, sickness, devotion, and love for that flag—Crittenden, American, was born."[18] The animosities of the past have been buried; the nation can proceed to a new unity. Furthermore, the war

had put to rest for a time the troublesome social problems of the day; it had brought together every social element in our national life—coal-heaver and millionnaire, student and cowboy, plain man and gentleman, regular and volunteer—had brought them face to face and taught each for the other tolerance, understanding, sympathy, high regard; and had wheeled all into a solid front against a common foe. It had thus not only brought shoulder to shoulder the brothers of the North and South, but those brothers shoulder to shoulder with our brothers across the sea. In the interest of humanity, it had freed twelve million people of an alien race and another land, and it had given us a better hope for the alien race in our own.[19]

Fox seems to suggest in such passages his awareness of some of the social, economic, and political struggles of the 1890's; and

he predicts the widening role of America in foreign affairs—
although with something of the expansionist pride in the spirit
of the age. There is even a hint of a new approach to the race
issue in American life; for, though the attitude toward the Negro
is paternalistic in the book—as it is, indeed, everywhere in Fox's
fiction—there is at least an ameliorative spirit and the recogni-
tion that things will never be quite the same as they were in ante
bellum days.

Nancy Huston Banks, reviewing *Crittenden* in *Bookman*, saw
Fox as presenting in the novel the contemporary South's attitude
toward the Spanish-American War. She also felt Fox had come a
long distance from his earlier fiction: *Crittenden* was "a more
universal story, not localized like the others." Clay Crittenden
was the exemplar of his race and region—"its romance and its
chivalry, both true and false; its noble sentiment and its absurd
sentimentality; its consistent physical courage and its occasional
moral cowardice."[20]

Jeannette Barbour Perry in *Critic*, on the other hand, admired
the descriptions of Kentucky but found the character portrayal
weak: "Judith and Phyllis are beautiful damsels . . . and one desires to be interested in them and in their fates. . . . They slip
away and elude one—shadowy, unreal—in the glowing Kentucky
light." Miss Perry thought the battle scenes were "Cranesque"
in detail: "But why war? Why anything except the beautiful
pastoral glimpses?"[21]

William Morton Payne did not consider the novel great, but
he thought it an advance over Fox's earlier stories. Payne noted
that Fox had taken the popular view of the Spanish-American
War. Though he did not doubt Fox's sincerity, he felt that the
reader who recognized the realities of the war and its aftermath
would criticize the lack of penetration in the novel. Nevertheless, "it is probably as wholesome a book as could be made out
of the material offered by our unfortunate war with Spain."[22]

That Fox did hold the prevailing popular view, particularly
the Southern view of the war, is abundantly evident. But he
also felt that the war could give new direction to American life
by stressing the unity between the sections that the Civil War
had shattered. In the North, this lack of unity was probably
not so apparent or was not so keenly felt; but in the South it was
still a troublesome fact. Before 1898, too many Southerners
lived as ex-Confederates; after the Cuban war, they thought

of themselves more as Americans. Whatever the war may or may not have done to the nation as a whole, it did give the South an opportunity to participate once more in a national effort of the federal union. The South was well aware of this achievement; and Fox, as a Southerner, reflected it. Poor as the book may be in a literary sense (and it is difficult to regard it now as any kind of advance over Fox's earlier, regional writing), it does stand as a testament to the new national cohesiveness which the Spanish-American War forged.

CHAPTER 5

Mountain and Bluegrass Renewed

I *Vigilantes at the Gap*

JOHN FOX'S investment of time, money, and energy in the real estate and ore possibilities at Big Stone Gap netted little financial return. The initial optimism of the boom days was never fully recaptured following the breakdown occasioned by the panic of 1893. Fox's experiences in the mountains with the mountaineers, however, as already noted, proved highly valuable for the writing of fiction. Moreover, tangential activities of bringing law and order to the Gap region in the 1890's provided another windfall of local-color lore that paid handsome literary dividends. For several years following the Spanish war, Fox turned for fictional and essay subjects to experiences gained with a local vigilante group of which he was a member in the earlier years of the decade.

The native inhabitants of the Gap region, both those in the valleys on the Virginia side and in the Kentucky mountains to the west, viewed the "furrin" intrusion of the 1880's and 1890's with mixed feelings. They were quite willing to profit from the sale of land and from the leasing arrangements made with the outside developers, but they were not inclined to accept easily the law and order that the new industrialists demanded. The mountain feud and the personal vendetta were still too much in their blood to be easily eradicated. For a long period after the Fox family arrived, there was considerable lawlessness at the Gap. Mountain feudsmen and local bandits combined to terrorize feeble law enforcement agencies. If arrested, these desperadoes were not always brought to trial; if brought to trial, they were seldom convicted; and, if convicted, they infrequently served out a sentence. Never had a prisoner been executed in that area; such justice depended on personal vindictiveness. The high individualism of the mountain clansman demanded that he take care of himself and that he ignore the law as much as possible.

The staid Virginians and bluegrass Kentuckians who moved into the Gap area during the economic boom were quick to realize the necessity for bringing some elements of law and civilization to the region before its industrial burgeoning could flower to the full. They soon saw, too, that the locally established law enforcement agencies were powerless to maintain order. So in 1891 several of the more enterprising and bolder spirits among the engineers and professional people formed a local vigilante group, the Home Guard, for the apprehension of criminals and the guarding of prisoners. All were educated men—many from Ivy League colleges of the East; and all were respected, highly literate citizens of the older communities from which they had come. They soon formed an effective force that succeeded after a time in curbing the wild impulses of the natives. Criminals were apprehended, feuds were broken up, and punishments were meted out despite threats of reprisals and daring rescues by friends of those arrested. Soon Big Stone Gap became one of the stablest communities in the mountains; and Wise County, Virginia, became a model for law and order long before other counties in the vicinity—particularly those over the mountain border in Kentucky—could boast as much. Once their work had been completed and the local citizens trained to respect the law, the Home Guard dissolved and legal processes were returned to the local constabulary.

The Fox brothers were among the group that formed the vigilante force at the Gap. Horace Fox, the engineer, was a lieutenant in the force; and James and John, Jr., were, for a time, active participants. The experience enabled John Fox to learn more about the mountain ways and provided incidents for a number of fictional and nonfictional pieces that found their way into print soon after the turn of the century.

II *Interpreting the Mountaineers*

Blue-grass and Rhododendron, published in 1901, is a volume of personal essays derived, to a considerable extent, from the vigilante experiences at the Gap. Four of the twelve pieces are directly concerned with vigilante activities, two of the essays deal with general discussions of the mountaineer, three report travel incidents that involved Fox while he was in the mountains, and three are bluegrass hunting sketches. Nine of the essays had been published earlier; only three were new with the book's appearance.

The first two essays, "The Southern Mountaineer" and "The Kentucky Mountaineer," contain thoughts that Fox often incorporated into his public lectures and represent the two most important nonfictional statements he ever made about the mountain people. Tracing the Scotch-Irish origins of the Appalachian inhabitants, he shows the sturdy individualism of the people, their honesty, their hospitality, their isolation—and also their illiteracy, their lack of thrift, and their suspicion of new ways. Fox's theory was that development in the mountains had ceased about the time of the American Revolution; for, cut off from the rest of the world, the newly established inhabitants had retained the ways of that era. Hence, when the Civil War came, these people knew allegiance only to the Stars and Stripes; their loyalties were still to the nation forged by the Revolution. Though some few who lived in the valleys owned slaves and supported the Confederacy, many a Union volunteer left the mountain areas to swell the ranks of the federal forces. After the war, isolation once again set in; but earlier animosities between families were now expressed with guns; and the mountain feud with ambush and vendetta came into full flower. Only in the 1890's with the coming of the railroads, engineers, lawyers, and entrepreneurs was the old isolation broken down and the old way threatened. Only in Fox's own era was the mountaineer effectively exposed to the outside world and his life pattern laid open to change.

In "The Kentucky Mountaineer" Fox argues that the Kentucky mountain folk bear some marked distinctions from their Southern mountain brethren. The Kentucky mountaineers often took to the valley areas, the better lands; and the people were better fed, better clothed, and more intelligent than in other parts of the Southern mountains. However, strangely enough, they were also more isolated: "As a result, he [the Kentucky mountaineer] illustrates Mr. Theodore Roosevelt's fine observation that life away from civilization simply emphasizes the natural qualities, good and bad, of the individual. The effect of this truth seems perceptible in that any trait common to the Southern mountaineer seems to be intensified in the mountaineer of Kentucky."[1]

Fox maintains the Kentuckian is "more clannish, prouder, more hospitable, fiercer, more loyal as a friend, more bitter as an enemy, and in simple meanness—when he is mean, mind you—he can out-Herod his race with great ease."[2] All of these qualities the writer illustrates with incidents and anecdotes from his own experience in the mountains or from stories he has heard. Fox, as noted earlier, was remarkably successful in getting close to the mountaineers, in breaking down their natural antipathies and suspicion of strangers, and in getting to know them as a friend. His essay in this instance is obviously that of a candid observer. He argues that the feud most sharply differentiates the Kentucky mountaineer from his fellows, but extreme isolation has made this relic of barbarism possible in the Kentucky mountains. And the feud means, Fox frankly notes, "ignorance, shiftlessness, incredible lawlessness, a frightful estimate of the value of human life; the horrible custom of ambush, a class of cowardly assassins who can be hired to do murder for a gun, a mule, or a gallon of moonshine."[3]

This bleak picture of Kentucky mountain life, however, is only half the story—though it is the portrait of the mountaineer generally publicized in the outside world. "There is another side and it is only fair to show it," Fox writes.[4] Although the Civil War was the chief cause of the feuds, clannishness was an inheritance that went back even beyond the American Revolution to the border disputes of old Scotland. And "whatever race instinct, old-world trait of character, or moral code the backwoodsman may have taken with him into the mountains—it is quite sure that that instinct, that trait of character, that moral code, are living forces in him to-day."[5]

Furthermore, a feud generally involved only a minority of the inhabitants of an area, although most might have sympathies with one side or the other. A code was pursued, too, in carrying out the feud: "The non-partisan and the traveller are never molested. Property of the beaten faction is never touched. The women are safe from harm, and I have never heard of one who was subjected to insult. Attend to your own business, side with neither faction in act or word and you are much safer among the Kentucky mountaineers, when a feud is going on, than you are crossing Broadway at Twenty-third Street."[6] Personal devotion is the code of the mountains, and there is no higher law. Feuding is bad, but Fox also points to the mitigating factors.

Finally, Fox underscores the hardiness of the race of mountain people he knows. Sons and daughters of pioneers of the Revolution, they have made as great a contribution to the development of the nation as the Puritan or the Cavalier. Only the sturdy Scotch-Irish strain that peopled the area could have survived the hardships and the isolation. A dour breed of men they are, perhaps, but a strong one and patriotic to the core.

Following the two formal introductory essays on the nature of the mountaineer, Fox turned to more informal sketches in the remaining pieces of *Blue-grass and Rhododendron.* "Down the Kentucky on a Raft," which appeared originally in *Scribner's Magazine* for June, 1900, and was his first publication with the house of Scribner's, is an exciting, authentic description of felling logs in the mountains of Kentucky and floating them down the Kentucky River in raft formation to Frankfort, the state capital. From Jackson in "bloody" Breathitt County, where Hell-fer-Sartain Creek flows into the middle fork of the Kentucky River, he proceeds down through the mountains, then the foothills, to the bluegrass region and Daniel Boone's country. This venture Fox had witnessed as a youngster, and he also related it in fictional form in several short stories and in his novel, *The Little Shepherd of Kingdom Come.* The essay records in lively tones an aspect of mountain culture that was colorful, though not indigenous to the region. "Logging" or rafting down the river was characteristic of a more primitive life in most areas of America, though it lingered in the Kentucky mountains longer than elsewhere. The essay is one of the finest Fox ever drew; the excitement, color, and even the technical details of descending the river compare favorably with any such writing in our literature.

"To the Breaks of Sandy," also published earlier in *Scribner's Magazine* (September, 1900), is concerned with another of Fox's travel adventures—a fishing trip to one of the most inaccessible areas of the East, the headwaters of the Big Sandy River near the point where Kentucky, Virginia, and West Virginia come together. Here the fishing turned out to be a disappointment, but the mountain scenery and the mountain folk in their cabins were to be observed. Fox does some of his best nature writing in the sketch; his love for the mountain regions is clearly evidenced in the perception with which he describes the country. The author and his companions also met several picturesque characters who appear in fictional guise in some of his later stories: for example, Melissa, a mountain maid of the sketch, was one of the rare but not nonexistent types to be found in the hills—a pretty girl with a pert way—and she could have served as the model for several of Fox's heroines from Easter Hicks of "A Mountain Europa" to June Tolliver of *The Trail of the Lonesome Pine.*

Five of the sketches are specifically concerned with mountain feuds and Fox's activities in the vigilante group at Big Stone Gap. "Through the Bad Bend" tells of another fishing venture through the mountains from Virginia into Kentucky and thence into the Cumberland heartland. Fox and his companion Breck fish their way downstream to the cabin of Uncle Job Turner, only to discover after they arrive there that they have passed through the territory of the "enemy," the Howard gang, since Uncle Job is identified with the opposing family and is the Turner who lives farthest up the river from his home base. Uncle Job also informs them that they have passed within a few steps of innumerable moonshine stills along the way, always dangerous territory for a "furriner," who may be regarded as a revenue agent. Though viewed with suspicion, they have been allowed to pass through the Bad Bend even with some degree of hospitality. The moral seems to be that one is safe enough in feuding country if he takes no sides and goes on his way minding his own business.

In "Civilizing the Cumberland," a factual account of the formation of the volunteer guard at the Gap, Fox points out that the railroad is ordinarily the first element of civilization to penetrate the mountains: "But unless the church and the school, in the ratio of several schools to each church, quickly follow, the railroad does the mountaineer little else than great harm. Even with the aid of these three, the standards of conduct of the outer world are reared slowly."[7] The mushroom growth of the 1880's and 1890's brought considerable disorder rather than stability to many of these mountain communities. The Gap was the one exception:

In this town, certain young men—chiefly Virginians and blue-grass Kentuckians—simply formed a volunteer police-guard. They enrolled themselves as county policemen, and each man armed himself—usually with a Winchester, a revolver, a billy, a belt, a badge, and a whistle—a most important detail of the accoutrement, since it was used to call for help. They were lawyers, bankers, real-estate brokers, newspaper men, civil and mining engineers, geologists, speculators, and several men of leisure. Nearly all were in active business—as long as there was business—and most of them were college graduates, representing Harvard, Yale, Princeton, the University of Virginia, and other Southern colleges.[8]

This part-time police force of young gentlemen who served without pay soon brought a unique peace to at least one mountain community: "The sternest ideals of good order and law were set up at once and maintained with Winchester, pistol, policeman's billy, and whistle. It was a unique experiment in civilization, and may prove of value to the lawful among the lawless elsewhere; and the means to the end were unique."[9] For one thing, moonshining was effectively regulated:

The first problem was moonshine and its faithful ally—"the blind tiger." The "tiger" is a little shanty with an ever-open mouth—a hole in the door like a post-office window. You place your money on the sill, and at the ring of the coin a mysterious arm emerges from the hole, sweeps the money away, and leaves a bottle of white whiskey. Thus you see nobody's face; and thus the owner of the beast is safe, and so are you—which you might not be if you saw and told. In every little hollow about the Gap a tiger had his lair, and these were all bearded at once by a petition to the county judge for high-license saloons, which was granted. This measure drove the tigers out of business and concentrated moonshine in the heart of the town, where its devotees were under easy guard.[10]

New town ordinances prevented the Saturday-night spree of wild riding mountaineers who used newly installed signs to test their somewhat unsteady pistol marksmanship: "The wild centaurs were not allowed to ride up and down the plank walks with their reins in their teeth and firing a pistol into the ground with either hand; they could punctuate the hotel-sign no more; they could not ride at a fast gallop through the streets of the town, and— Lost Spirit of American Liberty—they could not even yell!"[11] Bandits from the Virginia side and wild Jayhawkers who came over the mountains from Kentucky were dealt with in equally effective fashion by the Virginia cavalier and by Kentucky bluegrass types who came to the Gap to civilize it.

"Man-hunting in the Pound," originally an *Outing* article (July, 1900), relates the capture of the Fleming gang, a benighted family of mountaineers, who had hidden out at the Pound, a section of wild country north of Cumberland Gap. "The Red Fox of the Mountains" and "The Hanging of Talton Hall" are lesser pieces that describe incidents of vigilante activity in apprehending criminals in the Gap region. Both deal with notorious characters, unusual but nonetheless deadly, who were finally brought to a justice that had not been meted out in the history of that region. Indeed, Talton Hall was the first man hanged in Wise County, Virginia. And the Home Guard was hard pressed to prevent his friends from rescuing him from the law. These three sketches provide further documentation of Fox's experiences as a volunteer policeman.

There were also three bluegrass pieces in *Blue-grass and Rhododendron*, and all dealt with hunting and had been published in earlier form in magazines. "After Br'er Rabbit in the Bluegrass," "Fox-hunting in Kentucky," and "Br'er Coon in Old Kentucky" attest to Fox's familiarity with outdoor life and popular forms of hunting in the bluegrass region of his day. In every case, his knowledge of the hunt seems drawn from experience; and he relates the incidents with the love of an aficionado. There is also more than a tint of the Old South tradition: the ladies are fair, the men are gallant, and the "darkies" are humbly obedient. The sketches, which made their contribution to the "moonlight and magnolia" tradition that Fox's friend Thomas Nelson Page had long fostered, contrast rather markedly with the mountain pieces. For in the bluegrass essays Fox is writing of his first love, the Kentucky region where he was born and lived, the center of the cultured, sophisticated Southern gentry. In the mountain sketches, on the other hand, he is an interested outsider, at least at the time of writing; and he seems less devoted to the region.

The mountain portions of the book, however, remain its strength; in them Fox wrote at his best. Without flights of rhetoric that sometimes mar his other writing, but with a lyric aptness that fits his subject, he masterfully discusses his experiences about the Gap and interprets the mountain character. As the *Nation* reviewer noted, "His manner fits his matter—fresh and springing like blue-grass; sturdy and stinging like rhododendron. His book is a little masterpiece of evidence in a case profoundly interesting to Americans and others."[12]

III　*The Civil War in Fiction*

It is possible that John Fox intended to write his first fiction about the bluegrass section of Kentucky and that the accidents of environment and circumstances led him instead to depict the mountains in his earliest works.[18] By the first decade of the new century, he was writing of the aristocrats of central Kentucky as often as he was sketching the mountain people. *The Kentuckians* had already stressed the theme of contrast between the two groups, and *Crittenden* had presented a bluegrass type as the protagonist. Increasingly, he sought to interpret his own home region as the new century brought him into the full-time life of a writer.

When Fox changed publishers from Harper's to Scribner's, he thought of writing a Civil War novel with a mountain-bluegrass contrast once again. A comparison of the regions might be illustrated with a story based on the state's Civil War heritage. By February, 1900, he had started this Civil War tale—*The Little Shepherd of Kingdom Come*. He worked at it off and on for three years, devoting more time to it than to any writing he had previously done. By the summer of 1903 it was ready for serialization in *Scribner's Magazine*. Even as the story ceased serialization, Scribner's, for publicity purposes, sent out copies of the book printed from the plates of the original periodical publication. A complete book edition of thirty thousand copies was published on September 12, 1903; in October the London Constable edition appeared. Scribner's expected the book to do well from the beginning, for reception of the story in the magazine was enthusiastic. The publisher was not disappointed. It was Fox's best-selling novel; it may have been the first United States book to sell a million copies; and it is one of two Fox books still in print. Many a reader has gained some understanding of the Civil War drama from vicariously experiencing the sense of romantic adventure the work instills.

In the novel Fox tells the story of Chad Buford, a homeless waif, presumably born a "woods-colt" (illegitimate), who decides to flee the Black Mountain area of the Cumberlands after the death of his latest foster parents in a plague. Chad makes his decision in order to escape the clutches of Nathan Cherry who has vowed to apprentice the boy to make up for some debts owed him by Chad's foster father. Chad, with his dog Jack and his uncle's squirrel gun, wanders for a night and a day before he stumbles onto the Turner and Dillon families, other mountain clans living to the west of his home over the Cumberlands in the valley of Kingdom Come Creek. The Dillons prove almost immediately unfriendly, cunning, and mean. But the Turners befriend the young lad and take him into their rustic household where he soon becomes like another son.

The early chapters of the book describe Chad's life at the Turners; his friendship with Melissa, the daughter; his devotion to the mother, father, and elder brothers; and his early efforts at the "blab school" under the tutelage of the schoolmaster, Caleb Hazel, an Abe Lincoln type of minor character who is one of the best drawn in the novel. Incidents that add to Fox's total picture of the Southern mountain people are from an earlier era than that recorded in his first sketches. There is a certain subtlety and charm about Fox's writing at this point, particularly in a memorable little scene where he tells of the efforts of the boy Chad to save his dog Jack from execution under charges of sheep killing.

With the coming of spring, the Turners float logs down the Kentucky River to the "sittlemints" in the bluegrass; and Chad is taken along. After a first-rate description of this journey that harks back to the essay on the same subject in *Blue-grass and Rhododendron*, Fox tells how Chad gets lost in the town of Frankfort and misses the train to Lexington where the Turner group is to rendezvous to make the return on foot to the mountain fastnesses in the East. Fox never explains why the Turners go on without Chad, but the boy decides to walk from Frankfort to Lexington in the hope of catching up with them before they leave the following morning.

But, on the way, Chad meets Major Calvin Buford, an aristocratic blueblood and one of the local gentry, who is so taken with the boy that he invites him to his home and eventually persuades him to remain in his household when it is apparent that the meeting with the Turners and the trip back to the mountains have been missed. Soon young Chad meets the major's neighbors, another aristocratic bluegrass family, the Deans. Fox must have drawn Harry and Daniel Dean and their proud, phlegmatic sister Margaret from composites of some of his loved acquaintances of Kentucky days. They represent an entirely different type from the mountaineer people Chad has known. They live in a world that is glitteringly attractive but seemingly unattainable for Chad.

The boy makes friends of a sort with the Dean brothers who are his own age and with Margaret. But, when word gets out that Chad is a fatherless waif, the Deans' attitude cools enough to persuade Chad that, attractive as it may be, he really does not belong in the bluegrass world. So he slips out of the major's home one night and returns alone to the Turners in the mountains.

But the major has been intrigued with the thought that Chad Buford may be a relative. So he pursues the problem into the mountain world where he learns that Chad is actually the legitimate son of a Mexican War soldier who did not return from combat before Chad's birth and that Chad is really the great-grandson of the major's uncle, Colonel Buford, who was killed by Indians in the Cumberland Gap. Obviously, with such blue blood, the boy must be reared to the aristocratic tradition. Chad, however, refuses to return to the bluegrass until he is finally convinced of the need for an education; he then resolves to make his way in the world regardless of his birth. With the schoolmaster, he finally leaves the Turner home in the Cumberlands and goes to the bluegrass to study. With the proper genealogy established and with his quick native intelligence, Chad rapidly makes his way into the best circles of Kentucky society as the years pass. From their first meeting, he and Margaret Dean have been destined for each other; and their romance seems to flower, indeed, until the storm of the Civil War breaks over the land.

The second half of *The Little Shepherd of Kingdom Come* is a war book. The title, so appropriate for the first portion of the novel, seems incongruous for the second. Chad is suddenly no longer little; and his days of shepherding on Kingdom Come Creek seem far removed from the exigencies of war. However, Fox accurately and ably depicts the split in family loyalties that the Civil War brought to Kentucky: "Nowhere in the Union was the National drama so played to the bitter end in the confines of a single State. As the nation was rent apart, so was the commonwealth; as the State, so was the county; as the county, the neighborhood; as the neighborhood, the family; and as the family, so brother and brother, father and son."[14]

Inevitably, Chad struggles to make his own decision when forced to a choice: "If he lifted his hand against the South, he must strike at the heart of all he loved best, to which he owed most. If against the Union, at the heart of all that was best in himself. In him the pure spirit that gave birth to the nation was fighting for life."[15]   Slavery does not sway him; indeed, the tragedies of *Uncle Tom's Cabin* he does not believe: "Slaves were sleek, well-fed, well-housed, loved and trusted, rightly inferior and happy; and no aristocrat ever moved among them with a more lordly, righteous air of authority than did this mountain lad who had known them little more than half a dozen years. Unlike the North, the boy had no prejudice, no antagonism, no jealousy, no grievance to help him in his struggle."[16] Finally, Chad decides to join the Union cause—largely because, like most of the mountain folk, he has known loyalty only to the one flag and the one nation: "Chad had little love of State and only love of country—was first, last and all the time, simply American. It was not reason—it was instinct. The heroes the school-master had taught him to love and some day to emulate, had fought under one flag, and, like them, the mountaineers never dreamed there could be another. And so the boy was an unconscious reincarnation of that old spirit, uninfluenced by temporary apostasies in the outside world, untouched absolutely by sectional prejudice or the appeal of the slave."[17] As the war progresses, however, Chad fights almost as if he has made the wrong choice. His sympathies often seem more nearly drawn to the Confederates and their cause than to the side he has joined.

Chad's decision to join the Union Army crushes Major Buford, his mentor. And it strains the connections with Margaret Dean, whose father and brother Dan have gone with the Confederacy. Margaret herself is wholly Southern in her sympathies, but another brother, Harry, has been "contaminated" enough by their uncle Brutus Dean (patterned after Cassius M. Clay, Kentucky Abolitionist) to go with the Union.

Most of the war story takes place in Kentucky. Dan Dean joins Morgan's cavalry, and Fox carries the banner high for the daring, swashbuckling rebel leader whose exploits in the bluegrass he chronicles from a knowledge derived from stories heard as a child and from his reading. Chad joins an Ohio cavalry regiment. At one point in the story, he gallantly rides to save Dan Dean's life when Dan, captured, faces a federal firing squad under false accusation of being a bushwhacking guerrilla.

At another point, he chivalrously refuses to fire at Dan Dean when that worthy opponent is pursuing him in combat.

As the war grinds on, the Confederate cause becomes hopeless despite the gallantry of men like Morgan, his subordinate Richard Hunt, and Dan Dean. In the chaotic deterioration of the brother-against-brother struggle in Kentucky, guerrilla bands sweep in from the mountains to plunder. Eventually both Union and Confederate armies have to reckon with these guerrilla units that plague both sides. One of the worst of these groups has been formed by Daws Dillon, one of Chad's old enemies from Kingdom Come. At length, Chad is sent on a mission to capture Daws and his troop; but Daws, who learns of the plan, sets a trap for Chad's men. Chad is saved only because Melissa Turner—who has loved him these many years—comes in the night, through a rain storm, to warn him. Dan Dean has also learned of the impending conflict between the Yankees and the Dillon guerrillas, and with a rebel group he waylays both forces after Chad's detachment has overcome the guerrillas. Fox finally brings the Dean brothers, Harry and Dan, into personal combat in this scene. Chad, however, manages to escape to fight another day.

With war's end, Chad finds Dan in an abandoned hospital of Morgan's men in western Virginia and carries him back home across the mountains and down the Kentucky River to the bluegrass. Harry Dean comes back too, to be nursed back to health by his sister Margaret. Margaret Dean, learning of Chad's kindnesses to Dan and of an earlier exploit in saving Harry's life, learns to forgive and renews her love. She shows Chad how Major Buford, too, forgave him. The major died before the war ended; but, before his death, he had Chad's mother's remains brought from the mountains to be buried in the family burial plot at the major's home. He had taken a similar step with the old patriarch, Chadwick Buford, Chad's own great-grandfather who had died in Cumberland Gap. Chad learns that Melissa has died from pneumonia contracted the night she came to warn him of Daws Dillon's trap. As a kind of penance, he postpones his marriage to Margaret and starts off into the West to make a new life.

At this point, Fox makes a play on the "shepherd" and "kingdom come" of the title and embraces the expansionist spirit of the Progressive era in which he was writing: "Once again he was starting his life over afresh, with his old capital, a strong body and a stout heart. In his breast still burned the spirit that had led his race to the land, had wrenched it from savage and from king, had made it the high temple of Liberty for the worship of freemen—the Kingdom Come for the oppressed of the earth—and, himself the unconscious Shepherd of that Spirit, he was going to help carry its ideals across a continent Westward to another sea and on—who knows—to the gates of the rising sun."[18] But Fox also suggests that Chad will eventually return, marry Margaret Dean, and take over the farm of Major Buford.

Reviewers hailed *The Little Shepherd of Kingdom Come.* Most thought it was a good book, although not a great one. *World's Work,* which called it "an epic of a neutral state," noted Fox's knack at capturing the meaning of the Civil War to Kentucky.[19] Duffield Osborne in *Bookman* doubted that a first-rate novel could ever be created from actual incidents of history; nevertheless, *The Little Shepherd of Kingdom Come* was "pleasing, well-conceived, and well-written."[20] Both the *Nation* and the *Independent* noted Fox's freedom from prejudice in relating an account of a war that still invoked strong feelings on both sides. They admired also Fox's capacity to write moving dialect fiction at a time when the genre was fading in popularity among writers.[21]

The Little Shepherd of Kingdom Come, however, appealed to the reading public despite any decline in dialect fiction that may have been prevalent. Furthermore, the novel caught the heyday of the historical-fiction fad that dominated the tastes of American readers around the turn of the century. It was on the best-seller lists for 1903 and held its appeal well into the 1930's at least.[22] In 1916, Eugene Walter did a successful stage version of the novel; and a silent movie was made of the book in the 1920's. A perennial favorite with juveniles, this work has enjoyed the widest sale and probably the most extensive circulation of any of Fox's writings, even outstripping *The Trail of the Lonesome Pine* which is more of an adult novel.

Although Fox had written increasingly of the bluegrass country and viewed *The Little Shepherd of Kingdom Come* as another venture in a similar direction (two-thirds of the book centers on this area), the best part of the novel deals with the mountains of Kentucky. The first portion, especially the part concerned with

Chad the shepherd boy and his early life with the Turners, is praiseworthy. There are not many boys in American fiction more appealing than Chad—Huck Finn, of course, and certainly Tom Sawyer, but probably no others. Chad is believable, and he does not seem too virtuous for reality—as Major Chadwick Buford of the Civil War era does. Authentic color and dialect are recorded in the Kingdom Come scenes. But it is not only that young Chad is illustrative of mountain youth; he is the beau ideal of the youth-type in that hazy, nostalgic, mythical past of the *fin de siècle*. As Frank Luther Mott notes, "The story of a boy's fight against odds recurs again and again in the best seller list, and here we have an Alger theme transferred from New York streets to the Cumberlands."[23] The spate of boys books that characterized the late nineteenth century found fitting culmination in Fox's Chad who is as virtuous as Lord Fauntleroy or Ragged Dick without either of those young gentlemen's priggishness.

Yet Fox's sympathy with the bluegrass aristocrats and with the Southern tradition is everywhere apparent. It is clear that lineage, blood, and caste are important in this world. Major Buford, who sees great native strength in young Chad at first but who is convinced of Chad's superiority when he learns the lad's true ancestry, and the Deans, who stumble onto the question of Chad's origins and treat it with the greatest concern, reflect the emphasis of tradition and name in the bluegrass culture. Courtly Richard Hunt, who takes over from the equally courtly John Morgan following that leader's death in the Civil War, is another illustration of bluegrass manner. Polished, confident, poised, imbued with the spirit of *noblesse oblige,* these people reflect the best of the ante bellum tradition as myth, at least, would have it.

Indeed, Thomas Nelson Page never penned a more noble portrait of the ante bellum South than Fox does in the bluegrass portions of this novel. Though Kentucky was a state divided in its loyalties, the bluegrass section around Lexington abounded in Confederate sympathizers. And, for that matter, there was no state more Southern in orientation after the war than Kentucky which did not join the Confederacy while the war was on. Fox's depiction is historically accurate, as well as aptly rendered in this respect.

To be sure, the book suffers from the racial attitudes prevalent

in Fox's day. "Pickaninnies," "darkies," and "mammies" grace
a landscape suggested as picturesque. Such names as "Snow-
ball," "Rufus," and "Thanky-ma'am" reveal the Negro's role not
only as servant but as clown to the white masters. It is a soft
picture of slavery that Fox paints—perhaps more accurate than
a harsher depiction would have been; for slavery was milder in
Kentucky than in many other areas of the ante bellum South.
Fox's treatment of the Negro, too, is very much in harmony with
the prevailing tone of the Progressive era. Attempts to bring
about a complete rapprochement of sections had resulted in
the paternalistic, happy picture of the slave world that permeated
the national mind, North and South, by 1903. The language
and portrayals may seem offensive today, but they were not
meant to be so and are no more out of place here than in Mark
Twain's *Huckleberry Finn*.

Fox's love for the bluegrass countryside is also evident. In the
chapter "The Bluegrass" he digresses in a short essay on "God's
Country." The Great Mother herself "fashioned it with loving
hands. She shut it in with a mighty barrier of mighty mountains
to keep the mob out. She gave it the loving clasp of a mighty
river, and spread broad, level prairies beyond that the mob might
glide by, or be tempted to the other side, where the earth was
level and there was no need to climb: that she might send priests
from her shrine to reclaim Western wastes or let the weak or
the unloving—if such could be—have easy access to another
land."[24] From Boone's time to mid-nineteenth century the land
had seen the growth of a sturdy and intrepid race. A paradise,
the bluegrass was not only the proper place for a pioneer people
but a pleasure to behold:

The land was a great series of wooded parks such as one might have
found in Merry England, except that worm fence and stone wall took
the place of hedge along the highways. It was a land of peace and of
a plenty that was close to easy luxury—for all. Poor whites were few,
the beggar was unknown, and throughout the region there was no
man, woman, or child, perhaps, who did not have enough to eat and
to wear and a roof to cover his head, whether it was his own roof or
not. If slavery had to be—then the fetters were forged light and hung
loosely. And, broadcast, through the people, was the upright sturdi-
ness of the Scotch-Irishman, without his narrowness and bigotry; the
grace and chivalry of the Cavalier without his Quixotic sentiment and
his weakness; the jovial good-nature of the English squire and the

leavening spirit of a simple yeomanry that bore itself with unconscious tenacity to traditions that seeped from the very earth. And the wings of the eagle hovered over all.[25]

In recording so well the divided loyalties and family divisions of the war, Fox probably wrote from his own family history. On his paternal side, the Foxes had been Unionist in sympathy; but his mother's people, the Carrs, were pro-Southern. Fox's maternal grandfather was arrested during the late stages of the war for suspicious activity as a rebel sympathizer and was held in a Union prison for a time. Though Fox's own father did not participate in the fighting, he experienced the confused and heartbreaking division that characterized that part of Kentucky. From the father, John, Jr., heard of these things; and he also learned from him of the exploits of the celebrated John Morgan, Southern cavalry leader from Lexington. At one time Morgan's men had camped very near the home of the senior Fox at Stony Point. Indeed, Morgan lore surrounded Fox as he went to school and visited in Lexington in the years of his growing up in the bluegrass. In addition, he had read accounts of Morgan's troopers, their campaigns and their methods of fighting, that enabled him to write with authenticity. Fox avoided the mistake so fatal to many of the historical novelists of the era: bringing historical figures into the forefront of the story. Though Morgan is introduced, the reader catches only brief glances of the actual man. General Grant also appears fleetingly—long enough to strengthen the traditional image of the famous general and no more. *The Little Shepherd of Kingdom Come* is a good novel from the standpoint of history.

As fiction, of course, the book must be judged as only a popular success; it has no claim to literary greatness. The main characters are too good; the villains, inevitably wicked. Virtue triumphs; evil is amply rewarded with disaster. The love story is sentimental; the plot can be anticipated at almost every step. However, the portion of the novel recounting the story of the boy Chad in the mountain environment is movingly and effectively told. Some of the minor characters in the early scenes are well drawn. The reader is left with the impression that it is an exciting, wholesome story for younger readers. Adult tastes were titillated by it in 1903; since then, younger readers have enjoyed it. Only as a

juvenile can it live; and as a juvenile it will live. For the book
has some value yet for youthful enthusiasts of Civil War lore.

IV   *Additional Mountain Sketches*

Meanwhile, Fox continued to write mountain-dialect stories
for his lecture tours and for the magazine audience. "Christmas
Eve on Lonesome" appeared in the December, 1901, issue of
Ladies Home Journal; and "Christmas Night with Satan" was his
contribution to the Christmas issue (December) of *Scribner's
Magazine* in 1903. These two stories, combined with "The Army
of the Callahan" from *Scribner's* for July, 1902, and two other
sketches not previously published, were included in his next book,
Christmas Eve on Lonesome and Other Stories, in 1904. By
now, Fox's reputation was such that Grosset and Dunlap published a cheap edition of his latest book less than a year after
the Scribner's publication of the first. Later, in 1909 and 1911,
Scribner's again published these *Christmas Eve on Lonesome*
stories combined in a single volume with the *Hell-fer-Sartain*
sketches of 1897 and with four items from *Blue-grass and
Rhododendron.*

The five sketches comprising the 1904 edition of *Christmas
Eve on Lonesome and Other Stories* are a medley of the tragic
and comic, fiction and near essay, fantasy and reality. The title
story is a short sketch of a mountaineer who returns one Christmas Eve to his home on Lonesome Creek after release from
prison. Buck has come back to gain vengeance on the man who
betrayed him to the law; but, as he returns on the snowy evening and creeps up to the house of his enemy to peer in the window, Buck discovers that his own former sweetheart is now
married to the man and that the couple have a young child.
The scene of family felicity that he observes through the window
brings a change of heart to the embittered ex-convict; and, instead of killing his man from ambush as the mountain code
allows, he slinks away from the house, still unobserved, reconciled to leaving vengeance in the hand of God. The title of the
story assumes significance when the reader is told that no one
on Lonesome—not even Buck—knew that it was Christmas
Eve. So the story becomes a little vignette of the Christian spirit
with perhaps some symbolic meaning in the young wife and the
child portraying a madonna image. A slight sketch of only half
a dozen pages, it is the kind of thing Fox could do best.

"The Army of the Callahan," the longest story in the collection, is farcical humor—a somewhat different strain for Fox to pursue. Heretofore, the humor that characterized his shorter pieces had frequently been underlined by a note of pathos or even tragedy; in contrast, "The Army of the Callahan" is almost a slapstick burlesque. Based on a Civil War incident that Fox had heard at Big Stone Gap, it relates the exploits of a nondescript, tatterdemalion group of men hastily assembled into an army of the Confederacy to defend the property of Southern sympathizers at the Gap against Kentucky Unionist marauders from over the mountain.

Flitter Bill Richmond, a local storekeeper and a rebel, gets a warning from Black Tom, the leader of the mountain Unionists. In an effort to save his store and supplies, Flitter Bill cajoles the local strong man, Mayhall Wells, into leading the defending force by granting him a mock commission as captain from Jefferson Davis. Wells, who appears to be stronger physically than mentally, gathers his force at the Gap to prevent the threatened predatory raid of the mountain men.

During the night of the supposed enemy attack, Wells's force is alarmed by a rifle shot and a commotion in the dark. Thinking that an advance post of their "army" has been routed, the defenders flee pell-mell in the darkness down the mountain side, only to discover the next morning that the commotion they heard was caused when a runaway slave kicked a rock loose while climbing over Callahan's Nose, a prominent cliff in the Gap. The next day, when word of Lee's surrender arrives, Wells is relieved of his command of the Army of the Callahan in a mock note written by Flitter Bill; and he is given the privilege of leaving the county in twenty-four hours to escape arrest and court-martial for grave misdemeanors. "Captain" Wells leaves the county in disgrace; but Flitter Bill, who has encouraged him during the whole mock-heroic farce, sympathizes at the last and speculates that he will bring Wells back again.

The story is an attempt to burlesque current tales of Civil War valor. But it is not particularly well told and the humor seems strained at times. The portrait of "Captain" Mayhall Wells is, however, well drawn; and the reader smiles at the mock seriousness of this pompous buffoon who is the equivalent of the town clown. Fox's pen may have been sharpened in this instance by his knowledge of such types at Big Stone Gap during the boom time.

"The Pardon of Becky Day," the best work in the collection, is a sketch of a Northern missionary woman who brings an end to a feud between two mountain families. As she enters the home of Becky Day to ease that lady's deathbed sufferings, the missionary calls across the street to urge the widow of Jim Marcum to ask forgiveness of Becky lest the widow have a dead woman's curse on her conscience. The reader then learns that the Days and Marcums have been feuding since the time Jim Marcum stopped courting Becky Day because of untruths voiced against her by his present widow. Later, Jim married the widow, and Becky sought vengeance through her family. In the course of the conflict, Jim has been slain; another Marcum has come home from the West to avenge him; and Dave, Becky's husband, is preparing to defend himself. Becky, on her deathbed, finally forgives the widow who is enticed into the home by the missionary.

But as Becky dies, a smile of triumph crosses her face: "I know whar Jim is. . . . An I'll—git—thar—first."[26] Here, as in several of his best sketches, Fox brings out well the vindictiveness of ancient grudges, the meanness of lives pinched by years of frustrating hatreds, and the unyielding nature of feuds that frequently have their origin in some petty incident of the past. The story is really not one of pardon but of sardonic revenge. Becky, even in death, is comforted with the spiteful thought that she will finally get her man away from the widow.

"A Crisis for the Guard," a sketch written in the first person, is based on Fox's life with the volunteer police force at Big Stone Gap. When a New England teacher comes to the Gap to tutor the two brothers of the narrator for entrance to Harvard, the teacher is quickly introduced to the hectic life of his students, who, although they are only fifteen and seventeen years old, play an active role in the Home Guard. The youngest, known as "the Infant of the Guard," gets his man as capably as any older veteran. The New England tutor quickly decides to join the Guard himself for his own protection. In reading the story, it is appropriate to recall that Fox, a Harvard graduate, tutored and taught school for a time at the Gap.

"Christmas Night with Satan" is a pleasant little dog story about a little girl's pet that is led astray by a band of marauding sheep-killing hounds on Christmas night. Only at the last moment is Satan saved from the rifle of the sheepowners and returned to his mistress. The story is of the bluegrass variety, not a mountain sketch, the only one of its type in the book. Akin to the coon-hunting and fox-hunting sketches that Fox wrote elsewhere, it records life in the Southern tradition of "darkies" and plantations. The little-girl protagonist and the dog place the work in the realm of children's literature, however. Fox, always a dog fancier, is said to have been inspired to write the story by a desire to immortalize Thomas Nelson Page's Scotch terrier, "Satan." Uncle Carey of the tale was Will Carey of the *Century* magazine, a frequent visitor along with Fox in the Page home.[27]

Only "The Pardon of Becky Day" and "Christmas Eve on Lonesome" match the effectiveness of Fox's best sketches in the earlier *Hell-fer-Sartain*. Even in these two stories the human interest is paramount, not the local color. We don't really learn a great deal about the mountain people from these tales; hence they lack general significance in Fox's total work. But they were widely read and appreciated by his public which had now come to expect his mountain or bluegrass stories at regular intervals.

CHAPTER 6

Off to the Orient:
The Russo-Japanese War

I   *A Reporter in Japan and Manchuria*

F OR THE FIRST time, with the publication of *The Little Shepherd of Kingdom Come,* John Fox, Jr., achieved not only national acclaim but also financial security. As a writer of a best seller, he netted a far more sizable monetary return than he had ever known before. The collapse of the land ventures at Big Stone Gap had thrown him—and his brothers—into such dire economic straits that for years he had labored to get out of debt and to alleviate the financial distress of his parents. Writing to his brother James in the summer of 1903, he said that he didn't want to borrow another cent as long as he lived: "If I had forty children I'd pound into them from the time they were born two rules—don't borrow and keep out of debt. Debt has been the unspeakable curse of my life and I hope to God I shall live to see the day when I am out of it."[1] In August, 1903, shortly after the first edition of *The Little Shepherd of Kingdom Come* appeared, he wrote his family from New York: "It looks as though the future were going to be a good deal brighter than it has been for ten years."[2] In January, 1904, while on a lecture tour in the East, he wrote his father and mother at Big Stone Gap that he was contemplating a trip to Europe with Owen Aldis, brother-in-law of Mrs. Thomas Nelson Page. In the same letter he said that royalties from *The Little Shepherd of Kingdom Come* would be enough, after all debts were paid, to take the entire family back to Kentucky whenever it wanted to go.[3] Both the proposed European trip and the return to Kentucky suggest that Fox now felt financially secure.

Nevertheless, another opportunity was in the offing to add an even greater cushion to his economic stability. Scribner's in February, 1904, asked him to go to the Orient to report the Russo-Japanese War and to do a series of articles on his experiences. Though Fox was plagued by his old ill-health and was in a hospital in New York at the time, he readily acceded to the request because he felt he couldn't afford to reject the good offer. So the European trip was canceled, a return to Big Stone Gap was postponed, and he was soon on his way to the Orient "to see the world, improve in health, and make money."[4] When he sailed on the *China* late in February, he carried a letter of introduction from President Roosevelt which he felt would secure him "the good offices of anybody anywhere."[5]

The sea voyage did him good, though he was seasick part of the way and the glare of the ocean was especially hard on his weak eyes. In Hawaii, his first stop, he was impressed, if not shocked, by the racial mixtures he saw represented in the people. "Every possible human mixture of blood I had seen that day," he later wrote, "but of the morals that caused the mixture I will not speak, for the looseness of them is climatic and easily explained. I am told that after five or six years the molecules even in the granite of the New England character begin to get restless."[6] A "human crazy quilt of skins" was rapidly being created in the islands, and the distinctive Hawaiian was quickly becoming the vanishing patch in the quilt. Nevertheless, Fox carried away two appealing pictures of the islands—one of the Hawaiian swimmers, lithe and statuesque in symmetry; another of the laughing, bronzed youngsters of this polyglot world.

Arriving in Japan, Fox put up first at the Grand Hotel in Yokohama and then the Imperial Hotel in Tokyo. He was with a group of correspondents, including his old friend Richard Harding Davis of Cuban days, and all expected to go soon to the Manchurian front. Meanwhile, they set about observing the sights in Japan. Everything was in miniature in this strange land of unusual people. Fox was not impressed with most of the ceremonies of Japanese life:

This morning I saw the Mikado open the Diet—i.e. Congress—the House of Peers and the House of Deputies. He read his speech in a sing-song half chant with little whines every now and then that made me think of Ray [greyhound dog at home] wanting to get in at the gate. There was lots of gold coin and epaulettes and swords and ceremony, but I was not particularly impressed even by the Mikado. I couldn't see him very well but he was round-shouldered, pigeon-toed, and his waddle was anything but kingly. He has the face though of a graven image. Japan is about what the Japanese fans portray it— jin rickshas—little two-wheeled black buggies—bare-legged coolies, people stumping along on musical wooden shoes, women with babies on their backs—little trees—plums and pears and pines—little gardens, little houses—everything is little. The word "squat" will fit the whole of Japan—houses, country, trees, people.[7]

He ate Japanese dinners to the accompaniment of dancing geisha girls; he saw wrestling matches and went to the Japanese theater to sit in silence, mystification, and wonderment; and he visited shrines and temples and was impressed with the glory of cherry blossoms.

By April, Fox and his colleagues were growing weary of Japanese procrastination in giving them permission to visit the battlefront. They were beginning to wonder if any of the correspondents would be allowed to see a single big fight. To avoid the smells of Tokyo (Fox's nose was constantly offended by the Orient), he and Davis journeyed into the mountains to Miyanoshita for a few days. Despite some disappointments, he had learned to admire the little people of Japan and their little country; for, as he wrote his mother,

These are wonderful little people, and I never tire simply looking at them. And the babies—millions of them—strapped to the back of any relative from an 80-year-old grandfather or mother down to an 8-year-old brother or sister. I saw one girl baby on the back of a little sister—not more than a baby—and on the baby was strapped a doll! I haven't seen an angry look nor heard an angry tone since I've been in Japan—except among the foreigners. But they are terrible little people, too, in a fight. They are handling the Russians as though they were stuffed dummies and it looks as though this war might come to an end in a few months. Imagine an army of 400,000 men and every man just as willing to die as I am to live—literally. They care no more for death than for the breath of a South wind.[8]

Still he was disgusted at the delays the government foisted upon them, for they had waited in Tokyo from March until midsummer: "I don't believe any correspondent will ever hear a bullet or shell in this campaign. We are treated like children, nuisances and possible spies and I'd drop the whole business and go home—if I could, honourably. But I can't and must do the best I can. . . .I am exasperated and disgusted but there is no help for it."⁹

By July, Fox and Davis had given an ultimatum to the Japanese government that they would not stay after the seventeenth of that month. Finally, they were allowed to go with a group supposedly headed for Port Arthur. But they skirted the battle-front at Port Arthur and headed overland instead for a trek to within seven or ten miles of the Russian front in Manchuria. They were quartered in a walled Chinese town for a few days amid rain, mud, flies, and black fleas, to await a big battle which never developed. Later they were taken to Japanese General Oku's headquarters for an interview; and Fox again reported his impressions to his mother:

Day before yesterday we called on General Oku in a body. One of the Princes of the Royal House was there as a captain and sharing the hardships of the Japanese soldier and officer—a young, well-groomed young man who had been educated in Paris. If I mistake not, you will hear much of General Oku before this war is over. He is the most remarkable looking man I have seen among the Japanese. His face so held me as he walked towards us that I scarcely noticed any detail of his figure. In profile it is kindly, particularly when he smiles, but full-faced you see that he could be hard as steel and terrible as lightning. In repose, it has the sadness of Lincoln but his eye is as remarkable as I've ever seen set in a human head. It is rarely still, large, deep, luminous and could look, I think, through a stone wall. The reception was very formal and very courteous. Indeed with a few exceptions the Japanese have been most kind and most courteous.¹⁰

In general, however, Fox regarded the whole Manchurian assignment as a fiasco. The correspondents were not allowed near the very front lines of the firing, and they were so carefully superintended by the Japanese in all their endeavors that they felt frustrated at every turn. After less than a month on the Manchurian front, he returned with most of the other correspondents to Japan and thence immediately home.

II Following the Sun-Flag

Six articles appeared in *Scribner's Magazine* between June, 1904 and March, 1905, recording Fox's impressions of his travels. On April 15, 1905, Scribner's brought out in an edition of three thousand copies a book made up of the six articles plus one other chapter, "Lingering in Tokio," written but not published during Fox's adventure of the preceding summer. *Following the Sun-Flag: A Vain Pursuit Through Manchuria* records Fox's story of disenchantment with his Japanese venture.

"The Trail of the Saxon," "Hardships of the Campaign," and "Lingering in Tokio" describe visits to the Tea-house of One Hundred and One Steps and his acquaintance with the Maid of Miyanoshita. He learns the Japanese custom of arranged marriages, when, along with the other correspondents, he develops a fondness for a thirteen-year-old Eurasian geisha girl, Kamura-san, for whom the group had collected a stipend in order to send her to school. But reluctantly they have to admit defeat when it is learned Kamura-san is quite contented with the arranged marriage that has been planned for her. A wrestling match and a visit to Fujiyama also occupy his attention. The early chapters of the book display the same fascination with the quaintness of the Japanese that Fox had expressed in his letters home. They also indicate his feeling of uneasiness about the delay in visiting the war front and his growing sense of Japanese duplicity.

The last four chapters of *Following the Sun-Flag* are concerned with his experiences in Manchuria. He tells of sailing for Port Arthur with his Japanese interpreter Takeuchi and his horse Fuji. Equipped with all necessary supplies he is prepared for the rugged war-road ahead. But the tone becomes increasingly critical as Fox relates the correspondents' failure to view the battlefront at Port Arthur; their weary trek into the interior of Manchuria, following the "war-dragon's trail" on a fruitless chase after the Russians (whom they never see); their near incarceration in the Chinese walled village of Haicheng; and a final visit to General Oku, who, though impressive in appearance, turns out to be a master of deceit.

Fox shows ambivalent feelings as he contrasts Manchuria and the Chinese with Japan. He admires the Chinese and resents the Japanese manner of lording it over their Oriental cousins. But he finds the Japanese more efficient—and, above all, cleaner people:

I like this Manchurian land and I like the Chinaman. Both are human and the country is homelike—with its cornfields, horses, mules, cattle, and sheep and dogs. The striking difference is here, you see no women except very old ones or little girls. Here is the absence of that insistent plague—human manure—that disgusts the sensitive nose in Japan. The "fragrant summer-time" would have been a satire if it had been written in Japan. But there is no charm here as there is everywhere in Nature and Man in Japan. Besides the Chinese, here at least, are filthy in person and in their homes—the smell of the Chinaman is positively acrid—while the Japanese are beyond doubt the very cleanliest [*sic*] people in the world.[11]

Toward the end of the book his frustration knows no bounds, and Fox gives a backward slap of the hand to the Japanese officialdom that has toyed with the visiting correspondents so long, but prevented them from fulfilling their mission. "Of this war in detail I knew no more than I should have known had I stayed at home—and it had taken me seven months to learn that it was meant that I should not know more," he concludes.[12] His final word is a thrust at the way they have been misled, which he views as a reflection on the Japanese character as a whole:

Somehow, as Japan sank closer to the horizon, I found myself wondering whether the Goddess of Truth couldn't travel the breadth of that land incog. [*sic*]—even if she played the leading part in a melodrama with a star in her forehead and her own name emblazoned in Japanese ideographs around her breast. I think so. I wondered, too, if in shedding the wrinkled skin of Orientalism, Japan might not have found it even better than winning a battle—to shed with it polite duplicity and bring in the blunt telling of the truth; for if the arch on which a civilization rests be character, the key-stone of that arch, I suppose, must be honesty—simple honesty.[13]

Reviewers who took note of *Following the Sun-Flag* were generally disposed to view the book as a contrivance to meet an assignment. "Mr. Fox has made some very pretty copy out of his four months' stay in Tokio," reported the New York *Times*. "As a record of nothing at all, it is, in its way, an achievement," was *Spectator's* verdict. But both publications, along with such others as the *Nation*, *Critic*, and the *Dial*, found the sketchy, breezy tone of the work entertaining and generally recommended it.[14] Furthermore, an element of thinly disguised Anglo-Saxon racial pride while viewing the Oriental world placed it squarely in the mainstream of prevailing Progressive thought. Fox felt more at home in the Cumberland Mountains than in the Orient.

Viewing the whole experience a few months later from the vantage point of his home at Big Stone Gap, Fox wrote in the preface to *Following the Sun-Flag*: "No more enthusiastic pro-Japanese than I ever touched foot on the shores of the little island, and no Japanese, however much he might, if only for that reason, value my good opinion, can regret more than I any change that took place within me when I came face to face with a land and a people I had longed since childhood to see."[15] After the initial introduction to the strange, bizarre little land, he had been completely disenchanted. When the Japanese government presented him with a medal and a diploma from the Emperor of Japan in June, 1907, Fox must have accepted the honors with mixed emotions. Six articles, later collected in one small volume—not a good seller, at that—were small recompense for the failure of a mission. He never served as a correspondent again.

CHAPTER 7

Following the Trail of the
Lonesome Pine

I *A Knight of the Cumberland*

FOR A YEAR after his return from the Orient, Fox rested
from literary endeavors. Scribner's had published *Christmas
Eve on Lonesome and Other Stories* during his absence. He
had contributed an introduction to *A Southern Cook-Book*
prepared while he was overseas by his sister Minnie. But the
acclaim and the rewards of *The Little Shepherd of Kingdom
Come* enabled him to rest after his travels and to savor the
pleasures of best-sellerdom.

In the fall of 1906, however, he returned to his forte, the
mountain story, with *A Knight of the Cumberland*, published
first in three issues of *Scribner's Magazine* (September–November)
and then in book form in late October. The first edition of thirty-
one thousand copies included two thousand copies in sheets to
be sent to London for publication by Constable in December,
1906; for Fox's fame was now international and insured sale
of any new book from his pen in foreign editions. *A Knight of
the Cumberland* is a slight, even trivial long story or novelette
that contains as much humor as "The Army of the Callahan"
and as much color and local lore as "Hell-fer-Sartain." But a
more interesting feature is its foreshadowing of a much more
important work, *The Trail of the Lonesome Pine*.

In the story, Blight, a delightfully beautiful girl so named because no man could resist her, comes from the East to pay a
visit to the Gap. The day she arrives at the settlement, she becomes the object of solicitude from two men—Marston, a sophisticated young engineer from the North, and Wild Dog, a
rough mountain boy from the Kentucky side of the border.

Marston soon pays court to the girl in customary fashion, but Wild Dog holds his interest in shy abeyance. Eventually, Marston as one of the volunteer police at the Gap has to arrest Wild Dog for public drunkenness and thereby incurs the displeasure of the mountaineer who never forgets a grudge. Thus the potential rivalry between the two men is augmented.

Later, the narrator (apparently Fox himself) takes his sister and Blight over the mountain to "the lair of moonshiner and feudsman, where is yet pocketed a civilization that, elsewhere, is long ago gone."[1] Fox draws a vivid picture of the mountain cabin and its life when the three travelers spend a night along the way with an isolated family: "There, all in one room, lighted by a huge wood-fire, rafters above, puncheon floor beneath—cane-bottomed chairs and two beds the only furniture—[were] 'pap', barefooted, the old mother in the chimney-corner with a pipe, strings of red pepper-pods, beans and herbs hanging around and above, a married daughter with a child at her breast, [and] two or three children with yellow hair and bare feet—all looking with all their eyes at the visitors who had dropped upon them from another world."[2] Fox gives a good description, too, of mountain electioneering as he tells of the approach and campaign speech of the Honorable Samuel Budd in his exhortations to his new constituents in the mountains.

When Blight returns to the Eastern city after her visit, the lure of the mountain community is strong; and, after a winter's absence, she returns to the Gap the next summer for a July 4 celebration. In addition to the customary games, the local inhabitants traditionally hold a tournament in which mounted riders, carrying the colors of their ladies, attempt to throw an ash-stick weapon through a series of rings—an early custom that harks back to the Sir Walter Scott-tinged South. Marston is entered in the tournament, and so is Wild Dog, who has practiced all winter for the event. It appears that a contest will ensue over Blight's affections since she is to be the Queen of Love and Beauty for this particular tournament.

However, shortly before the tournament day, Wild Dog is barred from coming into the Gap because of too many drunken excursions into the streets of the town. The Honorable Sam Budd, a state senator who had originally sponsored Wild Dog and placed heavy bets on him, secures a substitute in Dave Branham, a friend of Wild Dog. When the day of the tournament arrives, the senator's champion (supposedly Dave Branham) appears in disguise as "the Knight of the Cumberland." The contest is held, and the Knight of the Cumberland wins. When commanded to unmask as he is about to receive his trophy from Blight, he dashes for freedom and makes good his escape, upsetting all before him, including Marston who has masqueraded as "the Discarded Knight." All realize that the Knight of the Cumberland has actually been Wild Dog in disguise—he has played the tournament for his lady's favor despite the town's injunction against him. The story ends with Blight's leaving the valley, apparently destined to marry engineer Marston. But, as her train creeps through a cut in the mountain, she glances up to take the last wave of the hand of Wild Dog, the Knight of the Cumberland, who has loved above his station and who turns reluctantly to resume his role in the hills.

In this story, one of the poorest Fox ever penned, the plot is pointless, and the characterization is overly thin. Marston foreshadows John Hale in *The Trail of the Lonesome Pine,* and Blight is very much like the genteel heroines of some of his earlier fiction. Only the actual mountain scenes save the book. It does have descriptions of mountain life and mountain customs that are authentically, if not too imaginatively, drawn. There is more dialect in the story than in almost any other Fox wrote. Autobiographical, too, it may have been—based, no doubt, on incidents at the Gap. It is difficult to believe, however, that Fox ever took the story seriously. He was merely having fun with a mediocre piece of fiction written along the way to his second best seller, *The Trail of the Lonesome Pine.*

As a hint of that work to come, *A Knight of the Cumberland* illustrates the contrast between the cultured Easterner and the unlettered but essentially honorable mountaineer. Blight, it is obvious, cannot return Wild Dog's affection in earnest; and he can express his regard only from the timidity of his inferior position. Despite his roughness, Wild Dog draws sympathy from the reader who cannot escape being taken with an essentially honest, though unknowing, illiterate. Wild Dog's affection is sincere, but he does not press his point. He must love only vicariously; he seems to recognize his way is not Blight's. Blight, for her part, is drawn to Wild Dog without realizing quite why it should be so. In the story, Fox makes no effort to cultivate his mountaineer; he leaves him alone with his feelings in the mountains, proud but unwilling to bridge the distance between himself and the outsider he loves.

In *The Trail of the Lonesome Pine,* on the other hand, the author redeems his mountain character. Writing of a woman, he brings her out of her world, polishes her and makes her a worthy partner for his hero, Jack Hale. It is a mark of the difference that the world of East and mountain cannot be reconciled in *A Knight of the Cumberland,* whereas in *The Trail of the Lonesome Pine* the innate goodness of June Tolliver makes her almost too good for the educated Hale by the end of the story. The plot situations of the two works are similar, but the plot developments are quite different. *A Knight* hardly suggests what *The Trail* might unravel. Within two years, Fox had considered the conflict of types more seriously and had presented a more meaningful solution of the problem than this earlier humorous but trivial story could imply.

II   *The Trail of the Lonesome Pine*

The Trail of the Lonesome Pine, serialized in *Scribner's* from January to November, 1908, and published as a book in October, 1908, was Fox's major attempt to describe fictionally the boom-and-bust days of the Big Stone Gap area and the adventures of the volunteer police force of that period. Interlaced was a love story that incorporated the old interest in the mountaineer and his ways.

John Hale, a bluegrass Kentuckian, is an engineer who has come to the Gap to develop the mining potential of the region. On a walking tour over Black Mountain into the valley of Lonesome Cove, he meets June Tolliver, daughter of Devil Judd Tolliver whose back-country creek land Hale is seeking for his mining ventures. Both daughter and father, after initial hostility to the "furriner," are converted to friendship with the young engineer; and Hale looks forward to buying portions of Judd's mountain land that is rich in coal.

From the beginning, Hale is impressed with June's natural intelligence and vivacity. He urges her father to send the girl for an education to the Gap across the mountain. Reluctantly, and only after considerable persuasion from Hale and the daughter herself, who has heard glowing accounts of the outer world from an older sister, Tolliver gives permission for June to leave the valley. Under Hale's tutelage, June begins her transformation from an unlettered mountain girl into a charming stock heroine. She attends the local Gap school and makes such progress with her studies that a larger sphere is carved out for her as time progresses. Eventually, she is sent to Louisville to learn society's ways with Hale's sister; then, with Hale's encouragement, she makes her way to New York to study singing.

Meanwhile, Hale's mining ventures do not prosper; for the coal strain at Devil Judd's turns out to be a false one, and the iron ore deposits on the Virginia side of the mountain do not materialize. European capital shies away from further investment. The boom breaks, and Hale is left with little means to finance June's continued education. Yet he scrapes together what he can and unbeknown to her—he has assured her that her share of her father's land holdings is substantial—manages to finance her education in the East. Trouble also comes to the mountains in the return of Bad Rufe Tolliver, a brother of Judd, who had gone West after an earlier brush with the law. His return bodes a renewal of the Tolliver-Falin feud that has long plagued the mountains.

June returns from New York a highly polished and sophisticated young lady. While she has matured and progressed in the social graces, Hale has retrogressed. He has allowed both his manners and his apparel to deteriorate in June's absence—so much so that she is taken aback at his appearance and wonders if she can renew her old relationship with him. Hale, in turn, senses that she has changed in her outlook and fancies that he can no longer urge a fulfillment of their tacit engagement that was entered into before she left the Gap for her last trip to the East.

June's return to the mountains coincides with that of Bad Rufe. Her uncle, determined to show his audacity and contempt for the law, rides into the Gap one day and wantonly kills one of the volunteer guards. Hale, as a leader of the guards, is forced to the chase. Eventually, he tracks Rufe to the Tolliver haunts and captures him. Rufe is returned to jail in Wise County, Virginia. During the trial—which is tolerated by the Tollivers only on the assumption that no jury will dare convict him—June is called to testify against her uncle. She has heard him say that he was going to the Gap "to get me a policeman." Largely on her damaging testimony, Rufe is convicted and condemned to hang. When Hale supervises the carrying out of the sentence, his pursuit of justice causes a break with Judd and with June, who finds that blood relationships carry a greater weight in this instance than affairs of the heart.

The hanging of Rufe Tolliver is conducted with great precautions to prevent a rescue by his own clan or his premature slaying at the hands of rival Falins. Rufe, the first of the mountain badmen to be brought to justice, is not the last. For his mortal enemy, the Red Fox, a strange Jekyll and Hyde type character who has been responsible for providing the tip that traps him, is found to be guilty of murder, is convicted, and is executed soon after Rufe Tolliver. Both incidents were based on fact drawn from Fox's own experience with the Home Guard at Big Stone Gap and reported earlier in two sketches of *Blue-grass and Rhododendron*, "The Red Fox of the Mountains" and "The Hanging of Talton Hall."

June's father, fearing a renewal of the open feud with the Falins who have been delighted and emboldened at Rufe's execution, moves West with his family. For a time, it seems that the two estranged lovers will not meet; but the book ends with a propitious reconciliation. Hale wanders again into the cove of the Tollivers for one last visit to their cabin, and coincidence has it that June has returned from the West at the same time. They meet under the lonesome pine on top of Black Mountain near where they had met at the beginning of the story. The passage of the months has caused June to regain her early affection for Hale, he professes his continuing love, and the two lovers are married by a local mountaineer friend and prepare to begin life anew in the Tolliver cabin in the Cumberlands.

As a whole, the book is melodramatic and strained. The overly sentimental love story is not saved by the realistic glimpses of mountain life. The chief characters are not well drawn, although June in her younger phase is more believable than as an adult. (Fox often wrote more appealingly of children than of adults.) Once she is civilized and polished, June becomes only the usual heroine of sentimental romance. As Agnes Repplier noted, "It is hard to forgive John Hale for sweeping June Tolliver—a passionate young savage—off to school and civilization, whence she emerges in silk stockings and French shoes, with the glorious contralto voice common, alas! to all heroines, and a taste for such shockingly bad pictures as 'enfin Seul.' "[3] The uncivilized mountaineers are better than the protagonists. The Red Fox, a combination of mountain philosopher, preacher, and sly murderer, is a tragicomic scoundrel of plausibility. Uncle Billy and Old Hon, a mountaineer couple who run a mill near the Tolliver cabin, are the clearest characters in the book. Fox paints them with a local-color aura that is wholly believable. Judd Tolliver, June's father, is also convincing and memorable.

Numerous incidents in the book hold together well and seem authentic, but the over-all plot is too sentimental, too circumstantial, and entirely too formularized to be worthy of much acclaim. Readers of popular novels of the first decades of the twentieth century enjoyed such standard fare; for today's adult reader, it cloys.

Fox continues his accomplished descriptive powers of setting in the novel. The first half of the book is the best precisely because the author dwells on a consideration of the mountaineers and their lonely lives. The author's botanical powers are again brought into play as he delineates the mountain forests and the flowers of the valleys. When he is moved to discussion of his characters and their emotions, he is apt, however, to descend to such bathos as the following attempt to explain June's reaction to her awakening love for Hale:

And June? Her nature had opened precisely as had bud and flower that spring. The Mother of Magicians had touched her as impartially as she had touched them with fairy wand, and as unconsciously the little girl had answered as a young dove to any cooing mate. With this Hale did not reckon, and this June could not know. For a while, that night, she lay in a delicious tremor, listening to the bird-like chorus of the little frogs in the marsh, the booming of the big ones in the mill-pond, the water pouring over the dam with the sound of a low wind, and, as had all the sleeping things of the earth about her, she, too, sank to happy sleep.[4]

The novel continues Fox's discussion of the mountain culture begun in the essays of *Blue-grass and Rhododendron;* indeed, some passages from the earlier sketches are transferred literally to *The Trail of the Lonesome Pine.* There is, for example, a passage on vigilante activities that harks back to "Civilizing the Cumberland." Speaking of anticipated local resentment at efforts of Hale's vigilante group to control the feuds, the Honorable Sam Budd, local political figure, tells Hale: "This feud business is a matter of clan-loyalty that goes back to Scotland. They argue this way: You are my friend or my kinsman, your quarrel is my quarrel, and whoever hits you hits me. If you are in trouble, I must not testify against you. If you are an officer, you must not arrest me; you must send me a kindly request to come into court. If I'm innocent and it's perfectly convenient—why, maybe I'll come. . . . The vigilante committee may be the 'vanguard of civilization' but it will have 'a hell of a merry time' proving itself."[5]

Also, Fox's notions about the meaning of the mountain isolation are again rehearsed. Budd notes the mountaineer cannot be judged by the standards of today: "You must go back to the standards of the Revolution. Practically, they are the pioneers of that day and hardly a bit have they advanced. They are our contemporary ancestors."[6] Arguing as the author himself did in the essays "Civilizing the Cumberland" and "The Kentucky Mountaineer," Fox's fictional character notes that isolation has kept the mountain people at a stage of development comparable to the Revolutionary War period. The mountain man was loyal to the Union during the Civil War, for example, because he recalled the Revolution and could fight for no flag but the one which he had pioneered. As "contemporary ancestors," the mountain people are the closest link the New World has with the Old. Fox suggests here an anthropological interest in the mountain folk that cultural historians and linguists later exploited to advantage.

There is a prescience, too, in Fox's depiction of the ruined landscapes the mining industry would bring. June Tolliver, soon after the mines have been developed at Lonesome Cove, strolls out beside the little stream that runs near the family home. She finds it already polluted with the dregs of excavations and tree fellings:

Its crystal depths were there no longer—floating sawdust whirled in eddies on the surface and the water was black as soot. Here and there the white belly of fish lay upturned to the sun, for the cruel, deadly work of civilization had already begun. Farther up the creek was a buzzing monster that, creaking and snorting, sent a flashing disk, rimmed with sharp teeth, biting a savage way through a log, that screamed with pain as the brutal thing tore through its vitals, and gave up its life each time with a ghost-like cry of agony. Farther on little houses were being built of fresh boards, and farther on the water of the creek got blacker still.[7]

Though Hale is an engineer, he has a conservationist's mind by the end of the story when he declares to June what he will do to restore the beauties of the torn landscape: "I'll tear down those mining shacks, float them down the river and sell them as lumber. . . . I'll stock the river with bass again. . . . And I'll plant young poplars to cover the sight of every bit of uptorn earth along the mountain there. I'll bury every bottle and tin can in the Cove. I'll take away every sign of civilization, every sign of the outside world. . . . so that Lonesome Cove will be just as it was."[8] In truth, the era Fox describes initiated the damage to the "lonesome coves" of much of the Cumberland that continues to this day to mar the landscape of the mining sections.

Many portions of the book are interesting for the mountain lore they discuss. Mountain dwellings, furnishings, food, and dress are carefully described. Mountain superstitions are noted. But along with their worst traits—feuding, a regimented way of life, suspicion of strangers—the better qualities of the mountaineers are presented: their hospitality, their pride, their keen sense of family loyalty, and their religious nature. Nowhere does he depict them as shiftless ne'er-do-wells; their native shrewdness and energies belie the popular image of indolence and ignorance. Given opportunity, many of them could emerge as bright, industrious citizens; and June Tolliver is the epitome of what the mountain people could become. We suspect that her brother, her cousin Dave, and her cousin Loretta might all have turned out equally well if removed from the isolation of their place.

It is apparent that, in removing June from her environment and providing the necessary educational and cultural opportunities for her intellectual and social growth, Hale assumes a kind of semimissionary role that Fox regarded as important for breaking down the barriers to the mountaineer's development. Furthermore, in matching June, the native, and Hale, the outsider, Fox suggests a blending of cultures that such missionary endeavor might promote. Earlier and later in his fiction, the author seemed to question the advisability of such matches. Easter Hicks in *A Mountain Europa* is killed before she can marry Clayton. Blight is too far above Wild Dog in *A Knight of the Cumberland* to take his interest in her very seriously. Later, two pairs of lovers in *The Heart of the Hills* sever their attachments to each other and return to their own domains of mountain and bluegrass. June Tolliver and John Hale, however, break the pattern set by these other stories as Fox fuses mountain and outside worlds in their marriage.[9]

The Trail of the Lonesome Pine proved to be one of the most popular books John Fox ever wrote. It was immediately applauded by the critics, most of whom thought it represented a distinct advance for Fox over his earlier efforts. The *Review of Reviews* liked the "intensely national note" the author had struck in the novel and was particularly impressed with Jack Hale as "the type of American life of which we are most proud, the vigorous, brave, energetic man of flesh and blood, who 'does things'."[10]

Such echoings of the Rooseveltian "strenuous life" were to be found in the *Outlook* commentary as well, where the writer found the story "full of movement, feeling, sharp characterization, and striking atmospheric effects." The *Outlook* reviewer felt Fox had captured the mountain people even more effectively than Mary Noailles Murfree: "In point of descriptive quality this story ranks among the best American novels." The reviewer made another observation that must have met with Fox's approval, for it caught his purpose in creating June Tolliver: he noted that the heroine's development was not so much a taking on of civilization as it was a bringing out of "the latent dignity, independence, and ability inherent in her own nature."[11]

Ward Clark in *Bookman* intimated Fox was only following Murfree in exploiting the local color of the Cumberland. "His stories read very much like those of twenty years ago, when the hunt for Local Colour was at its height. His is the formula of those days, and he wins success by his courageous refusal to depart from it." Nevertheless, Clark acknowledged that Fox knew well the kind of people he wrote about and that whatever weaknesses he possessed were those of the local colorists in general: "It is as a novelist of manners of an arrested civilization that he scores his success."[12] The *Nation* reported that the story was melodrama—but "melodrama of so high a grade, so joyous an enthusiasm, and so compelling an interest as to give its reader an hour of uncritical pleasure."[13] The *Independent* and the New York *Times* were also impressed with a story that, the *Times* said, had "a new sense of reality and a very winning charm."[14]

From the first, the public took to the book; and it sold well. There was an advance sale of one hundred thousand copies on the first edition and a second printing was immediately forth-coming. Mott lists *The Trail of the Lonesome Pine* as a best seller for 1908, indicating a sale of at least seven hundred and fifty thousand copies for the decade in which it was published.[15] All in all, eight editions of the book appeared between publica-tion and 1936; and it is safe to say that by the sixth decade of the twentieth century it had passed the two million mark. It is one of two Fox novels still in print in a Grossett and Dunlap edition.

A few years after the book's publication, a successful stage version of the story opened at the New Amsterdam Theater in New York, January 29, 1912. The play, adapted by Eugene Walter, starred Charlotte Walker and W. S. Hart. Berton Churchill also appeared in this earliest version. Later, the Poli Players did *The Trail of the Lonesome Pine* in 1915 and 1919, and the Orpheus Players performed it on Broadway in 1922. Cinema versions of the book occurred in 1916, 1922, and 1936 (all made by Cecil B. De Mille), the last featuring Fred Mac Murray, Henry Fonda (in one of his earliest roles), and Sylvia Sydney. A popular song bearing the name of the novel titillated American ears for decades. For the song title, Fox apparently failed to get the royalty rights to which he felt entitled, but withal *The Trail* made his popular reputation and his literary fortune supreme. It is the Fox book best remembered even now. Today, at Big Stone Gap, Virginia, in the summertime a local theatrical group performs a musical version of *The Trail* in an outdoor theater beside the "June Tolliver House" where the mountain girl supposedly boarded when she first came into the Gap to go to school at Hale's urging. And the state of Virginia has de-signated a highway running through Big Stone Gap and Lee and Wise counties, paralleling the state line, as "The Trail of the Lonesome Pine."[16]

Very soon, too, public interest in Fox's novel sparked rumors over possible prototypes for the characters; and such speculation has continued unabated through the years. Though Fox during his lifetime denied most of the conjecture, there is no doubt that actual people did inspire his depiction of some of the characters. Rufe Tolliver was patterned after Talt Hall who "killed him a policeman." The Red Fox, preacher, 'yarb-doctor, and murderer, was a celebrated mountain character of the region, Doc Taylor, who wore moccasins with the heels forward so that no one could tell which way he had gone and who preached his own funeral sermon the day before he was hanged.

A writer in the Louisville *Courier-Journal* in June, 1949, maintained that Devil Judd Tolliver was modeled on Devil John Wright who had supposedly fought on both sides in the Civil War. A fabulous figure, Wright had killed thirty-two men and sired thirty-one children. When Fox knew him, he was serving as a Kentucky peace officer and helping the Consolidation Coal Company buy up land options in Letcher and Pike counties, Kentucky. June Tolliver, the same writer maintained, was June Morris, a mountain girl of the community; and Jack Hale was a composite of three persons, one of whom was Rogers Clark Ballard Thruston, a Louisville geologist Fox knew well.[17] It is noteworthy, too, that Hale bears some similarities to Fox's engineer brother, James. Still other speculations can be heard in the Big Stone Gap area to this day.[18]

The question of the lonesome pine tree's existence has also intrigued readers and visitors to the Gap. Actually, there was such a tree in the vicinity that grew so high up on the mountains, well above the usual range for pine trees, that it had some local fame while Fox lived there. Like Hale, "from the beginning it had a curious fascination for him, and straightway within him—half exile that he was—there sprang up a sympathy for it as for something that was human and a brother."[19] Hale had seen the tree "giving place with sombre dignity to the passing burst of spring—had seen it green among dying autumn leaves, green in the gray of winter trees and still green in a shroud of snow—a changeless promise that the earth must wake to life again."[20]

But Fox never saw the lonesome sentinel that gave title to his story. In 1910, he wrote an article for *Scribner's Magazine* describing a trip taken back into the mountains with a land agent to find the celebrated lone pine tree that rumor had placed in several locations. After trying unsuccessfully to find local guidance to the exact locale, the travelers met Uncle Hosea (Hosey) Bowlin, the only person yet living who knew where the tree could be found. But Uncle Hosea was up in his nineties and too ill to guide them to the lonesome pine. "I am still waiting for Uncle Hosea to improve, and if he ever gets strong enough, I shall strike that trail again," Fox wrote.[21] The tree was destroyed by lightning before he ever got around to viewing it.

CHAPTER 8

The Continuing Theme:
The Heart of the Hills

I *Marriage and Divorce*

BY 1908, John Fox's reputation had reached its zenith. Two best selling novels in a five-year period had assured him a prominent place in the contemporary literary sun. Moreover, he was able to move more freely in a social sphere commensurate with his newly won fame. From Harvard days on, he had enjoyed the company of journalists, artists, musicians, and people sometimes of a wealthier position than he could aspire to. In the early years in Kentucky and later in the mountains in Virginia he had known economic deprivation. Occasionally, after the panic of 1893 it had been necessary for him to borrow money to fulfill what he felt were obligations to his family and others. But at no time had he lost his sense of culture, his pride, or his desire for the life that fame and money might bring. So, when good fortune came to him in the first decade of the twentieth century, he was ready to move in appropriate circles.

Although Fox found his literary world in the mountains, and Big Stone Gap was always home after 1890, the lure of the cities was an enticement he could never escape. Increasingly after 1900 Louisville, Washington, and especially New York were havens of good company and entertainment. Fox's friendships with such people as Theodore Roosevelt, Thomas Nelson Page, Finley Peter Dunne, and Richard Harding Davis brought him into a society he loved. He visited in the homes of Page and Davis for weeks at a time, and he was an occasional guest at the White House, where, as noted earlier, he sometimes played his guitar and sang mountain songs or recited mountain dialect stories for the President's company. Fox also loved the theater, and music was in his blood. So it was not uncommon to see him at the theater or the opera whenever he made his frequent, extended visits to New York.

Indeed, it was from associating with theater folk and members of the world of music that Fox met his wife. There had been many light flirtations in Fox's life before 1908. One novel, *The Little Shepherd of Kingdom Come,* had been dedicated to an early sweetheart, Currie Duke of Louisville. His natural gaiety and charm of manner assured him an entree into the society of women. But only the glamorous singer Fritzi Scheff ever convinced him of the values of matrimony.[1]

Fritzi Scheff, native of Vienna, was a celebrated figure in her own realm in 1908. Her mother had been a prima donna of Wagnerian opera in Europe; her father was a celebrated Austrian physician and scientist. Brought up in the world of European music, she had sung leading operatic roles abroad and had appeared before Queen Victoria at Covent Garden, London. She made her American debut in *Fidelio* at the Metropolitan Opera in December, 1900. Gradually she had moved from grand opera to comic-opera roles. In 1906 she dazzled New York in *Mademoiselle Modiste,* the Victor Herbert operetta that had been composed partly for her. A great personal triumph on the stage, she spoke four languages fluently and was the belle of the city's musical world. She had already shed one husband, a young Austrian army officer, by the time she met Fox in 1908.

Newspaper reports of the time stated that Fritzi met Fox after sending him a note of congratulation on *Hell-fer-Sartain.* The meeting occurred at the home of their mutual friend, Finley Peter Dunne; later Fox became a regular guest at her Sunday night receptions at the Savoy Hotel whenever he was in New York. Their engagement was announced by the press in September, 1908; and they were married on December 13, 1908, at the home of Fox's brother, Rector Fox, in Mount Kisco, New York. The wedding was a quiet one with only a few friends in attendance; but, as was to be expected, it inspired news stories and comments in many of the daily publications of the time. It was noted that Fritzi Fox (the name never really caught on!) intended to continue her career, while the author would pursue his writing at his leisure.

Apparently, leisure was not quickly to be had in Fritzi's company. Known for her temper tantrums, Fritzi was called "the little devil" in the theater (a name supposedly given her by Paderewski) and was celebrated for her eccentricities. She traveled like an Oriental potentate in her own railcar with a retinue of attendants and dogs. She loved luxury and admitted it. Reports had it that on one excursion she pulled the emergency cord on a train so it would stop and not spill her bath water. Another time she feigned illness in Cleveland, then sat in the audience and grated her teeth while an understudy sang her role. Her whimsical ways caused her to break with several managers by 1912, including Charles Dillingham, the Shuberts, and Joseph Gaites. When she finally became her own manager in 1913, her company failed; and she eventually reached a state of financial crisis brought on largely by her own ignorance of monetary management.

Into this maelstrom of a career Fox was thrust by his marriage. Small, suave, quiet, and more like a typical Englishman than an American in manner, Fox enjoyed theatrical folk and the life of the theater; but he could hardly have been prepared for Fritzi Scheff. For a time he accompanied her on her concert tours. And she came to Big Stone Gap rather frequently during their marriage to rest and entertain the natives. Entertain she did—she sang, played golf and tennis, rode horseback, went for drives, helped finance a local baseball team, and threw lavish parties for all comers. One Christmas she interrupted her tour to return to the Gap to play Santa Claus to the local children. Her birthday, August 30, became a day of local celebration. The "Fox place" rang with song and became a center of activity whenever she was in town. Her mother, a German lady who spoke little or no English, was also on hand to inspire the local citizens on occasion. All in all, Fritzi Scheff brought an air of cosmopolitanism to the little mountain community that it had never before enjoyed and has seldom seen since.

For both parties, however, the marriage was an ill match. Fritzi was too wedded to her career really to take marriage seriously. Temperamentally, she was unsuited to a stable domestic relationship. For his part, Fox soon tired of serving as impresario to a prima donna. He had his own work to do and following in Fritzi's retinue gave him little time to pursue it. Finally, in February, 1913, they were divorced. Still on friendly terms, they had altogether different careers which they were unwilling to push aside to save their marriage. Fritzi Scheff went her way to con-

tinue in the theater, though her musical career declined after
1912. Appropriately enough, she went into vaudeville eventually,
where she had other triumphs.

II *Magazine Sketches*

Meanwhile, Fox's literary output dwindled to five articles during his marriage, although *The Heart of the Hills,* a novel he
had worked at spasmodically for several years, was serialized in
Scribner's beginning in the spring of 1912 and was finally published in March, 1913. "Christmas Tree on Pigeon" was published in *Collier's,* December 11, 1909, and was included later
in the volume of collected stories entitled *In Happy Valley.*
The four other articles made up a series in *Scribner's Magazine*
for August, September, October, and December, 1910, and
were never published elsewhere.

The first three of this series capitalized on the vogue of Fox's
earlier work in that each was an informal essay-type account of
an actual visit to some of the locales previously dealt with in his
fiction. "On Horseback to Kingdom Come," the first of the
three, for example, tells of "going over to see Kingdom Come
[Creek] with the eyes of his body instead of his mind."[2]
After crossing from the Gap to Whitesburg in Letcher County,
Kentucky, Fox proceeds to the headwaters of the stream he had
immortalized in his story of Chad Buford. Here he finds a family
named Frazier, descendants of the first settlers there, who might
well have been models for the Turners. And he finds a boy who
plays mountain tunes just like Chad and a girl who could have
posed for Melissa.

Things are different now in the mountains, more civilized than
what he recollects from earlier visits in the 1880's and 1890's:
"The log-cabin was no more. The houses were tidy, weather-
boarded, and painted; men were ploughing industriously in the
fields; I passed children in the road, no longer in tatters, and
with school-books in their hands, and not a soul asked who I was
and what I was doing over there. Evidently a stranger was no
longer a rare bird along that creek; curiosity was slack and suspicion was gone."[3] More important, feuding has all but disappeared. He finds, too, that people have read his book, *The
Little Shepherd of Kingdom Come,* and liked it. This appreciation had not always existed: "I recalled having no little trouble
over my first book about the mountaineers, of just escaping a

'rough house' at the hands of some students of a mountain college, and of being often charged by educated mountaineers that I had not done them justice, and by 'furriners' of having given the mountaineers credit for more than was their due."[4]

"On the Road to Hell-fer-Sartain" (September, 1910) and "On the Trail of the Lonesome Pine" (October, 1910) record similar visits into the mountains to find sites that Fox had previously used in his stories. On his visit to Hell-fer-Sartain Creek he attends a mountain preaching, where members of the congregation come and go at will; and he also hears a new version of the origin of the stream's name. In his story, "Hell-fer-Sartain" was derived from the fighting character of the dwellers along its bank. But now he meets an old mountaineer who tells him: "Folks say an old bear hunter goin' up the creek met another one coming down. 'Whar'd you come from?' he says. 'I come down a devil of a place,' t'other feller says. 'Well,' says the first man—'you're goin' into hell fer sartain now.' "[5] Once again Fox notices signs of universal change in the mountains, although feuding has not altogether vanished around Jackson in "bloody" Breathitt County.

"Christmas for Big Ame" in *Scribner's,* December, 1910, catches the spirit of the season in narrating Marshal Hawkins' trip into the mountains to arrest Big Ame, a notorious moonshiner, who has previously shot and wounded him. He stops during a snowstorm on Christmas Eve at the cabin of a mountain woman who tells him of recent events in the life of Big Ame. It seems Big Ame earlier had loved Melisse Phillips, but she followed a traveling salesman to Norfolk. Later Big Ame pursued her to the city, and had finally found her, alone and deserted, with her baby in a hospital. He has now brought her back to the mountains and married her, adopted the baby as his own, and given up his moonshining. On hearing the account of the mountaineer's reformation, the marshal tears up the warrant in a gesture that serves as a Christmas present for his old adversary. This one sketch of the four in the *Scribner's* series may be more fiction than fact, although Fox often used true incidents as the basis for fictional embroidery in his work.

III   The Heart of the Hills

Such magazine writing was ephemeral, but *The Heart of the Hills* was another major effort. The novel was dedicated to Fox's father who died in 1912. The senior Fox had often helped the author by making suggestions of phraseology and by supplying factual data for many of his stories. Fox relied heavily on his old teacher for guidance in the Classics and for material that might ordinarily have required the substantiation of an encyclopedia or reference book. The father's loss was a heavy blow to the son for this reason, as well as for the breaking of the close bond of affection that held them.

The Heart of the Hills is a hill-country story and also an interesting contrast of bluegrass and mountains. In some respects, it reminds the reader of the earlier *Little Shepherd of Kingdom Come;* on the whole, it is a poorer book and never enjoyed the popularity of *The Little Shepherd.* Nevertheless, Jason Hawn is one of the best fictional portraits Fox ever drew. Jason, who grows up in the mountains, lives with his widowed mother, a member of the rival Honeycutt clan. Jason's father had crossed his own tribe by marrying a Honeycutt, and it was assumed that one of his own people might have killed him because of his apostasy. Jason and his mother live just over the ridge from Steve Hawn and his daughter, Mavis. Steve has taken an interest in the widowed mother of Jason, which does not please young Jason who still nurses a fondness for his father that includes a pledge of revenge on the father's assassin. But he must tolerate the courtship since his mother is not inclined to reject it.

Jason and Mavis, second cousins, grow up together. They play together, fish together, and roam the woods in their few moments of idle time. One day they encounter two strangers of about their own age who have come from the bluegrass into the mountain country: Gray and Marjorie Pendleton, cousins of notable lineage, who have accompanied Gray's father, Colonel Pendleton, into the mountains to see about the purchase of some coal-mining areas. The contrast between the two couples— the mountain children and the genteel bluegrass cousins—is one of the dominant themes of the book.

After their initial hostility, it is apparent that the four are going to become fast friends. Shortly, Mavis is taken from the hills by her father when he elopes with Jason's mother and goes to the bluegrass to find work and to escape the wrath of the Hawn-Honeycutt feud. Soon, too, young Jason decides to go to school in the bluegrass. At the urging of a teacher he has met earlier in the mountains, he goes to the university in Lexington

(though the city is never named) to matriculate. Mavis, his
mother, and his new foster father, Steve Hawn, are nearby. So
is Marjorie Pendleton; and, as the months pass, Jason finds
himself drawn to her, and she, for reasons quite beyond her
comprehension, has a strong sympathy for him. His youthful
enthusiasm and wild abandon, his desire to learn proper etiquette
and the manners of the outside world, appeal to her. And he is
moved by her charm, decorum, and genteel pattern of behavior.
Gray Pendleton and Mavis Hawn are likewise attracted to each
other. Fox is keenly interested in these contrasting types with
all the suggested nuances. Though the reader suspects that such
matches are not to be sanctioned, these two couples find themselves slipping from fondness into love, and eventually marriage
looms as a distinct possibility for both pairs. To forestall this
possibility, however, Fox sends Mavis and Jason back to the
hills where they are truly more at home and keeps Gray and
Marjorie for each other, as intended by their parents all along.

The novel proceeds smoothly enough as long as it continues in
this vein of contrasting types and salubrious love stories. It picks
up momentum and interest, however, when Fox brings political
and economic issues into play. The main action of the story occurs
around 1900. In that year, William Goebel, a Bryan Democrat
and political power in the state of Kentucky, was assassinated in
Frankfort, the state capital, by unknown persons supposedly of
Republican leanings. Since Republicanism was centered in the
eastern mountains, it was assumed mountaineers were responsible.
Goebel had just recently been narrowly defeated in a disputed
election for the governorship by the Republican candidate. The
Democrats had charged a "stolen" election and, through their
leadership in the legislature, were challenging the legality of the
contest. The assassination of Goebel set off another outcry of
corruption and political machination. For a time the state was
thrown into virtual civil war. Finally, the elected governor,
Taylor, had to leave Kentucky for Indiana when federal courts
upheld a lower court decision awarding the governorship to
J. C. W. Beckham, a Goebel man who was re-elected on his
own in 1903. The Republicans claimed "they stole the election,"
and the Democrats charged that "they killed our Governor," but
no one knows to this day who shot Goebel.[6] The affair was one
of the most disturbing in all Kentucky political history.

It is this incident that Fox weaves into his story. Jason Hawn,

student at the university, is angered by the turn of events at the
capital, considers the dangers of an election stolen from the
mountain people, and joins a large group of them as they assem-
ble in the capital to preserve their rights. At the time the political
leader he opposes (obviously Goebel) is assassinated, he and
his step-father, Steve Hawn, are in the capitol building. When
they are suspected of having a part in the assassination, they
flee to the hill country to escape the law. Eventually, Jason is
caught, quickly tried, and released. Steve's role is more am-
biguous, but he finally eludes conviction too. In his struggle with
authority, Jason is aided by Gray Pendleton and Gray's father
who see the duplicity of the reigning Democrats in the state.

Kentucky's so-called Tobacco War of the turn of the century
is also introduced into the story. Steve Hawn, a ne'er-do-well
who is frequently in the midst of strife and underhanded trouble,
rides out with the new night riders to fire the fields of those
tobacco growers they oppose. Colonel Pendleton's crop is saved
by Jason and Gray after a forewarning from Jason's mother. Fox
does not argue the economics of the issue in the book, but his
sympathies in the narrative are clearly on the side of those owners
who wished to grow tobacco and sell it on the open market as
opposed to the group who wished to conduct a boycott in protest
against the trusts.

At the end of the book Jason goes back to the hills to regain
the land he had been deprived of when his mother sold his
property to Colonel Pendleton for coal exploitation. Jason will
conduct the new mining interests that Gray Pendleton has form-
erly managed while Gray goes back to the bluegrass to manage
his father's estate. The book concludes with the marriage of
Jason and Mavis who will make their home in the mountains;
Gray and Marjorie are united to join the two families of the
bluegrass.

The first part of *The Heart of the Hills* contains a view of
mountain life and of a mountain waif similar to the early pages
of *The Little Shepherd of Kingdom Come.* Jason Hawn is a
better developed character than Chad Buford of the earlier
book, and he is not so annoyingly perfect as Chad. Jason never
quite overcomes a streak of bad temper, and he can be as stub-
born as the worst mountain man on occasion. Also, his development from childhood to adulthood is more perceptively sketched.
In *The Little Shepherd,* Chad seems to jump overnight from

youth to maturity. As a youngster, he roams the hills; but, when Fox gets him to the bluegrass, the Civil War quickly comes and he is an adult. But in *The Heart of the Hills* Jason moves almost imperceptibly from the thoughts and moods of a boy to those of an adult without at the same time losing the pensiveness that seemed to characterize the younger children in the mountain communities.

Mavis is also well done. She is something like June Tolliver in *The Trail of the Lonesome Pine* and certainly is as perceptive in her view of life as June ever became. It is interesting to note that both girls are awakened and brought to a full realization of their talents when they leave the hills, but both return to find their destinies in the land of their fathers. As Frederic Cooper stated in a *Bookman* review of *The Heart of the Hills:* "What Fox seems to say . . . is that Cumberland Mountain folk possess as fine qualities as any if they have contacts with the fine aristocracy of the Blue-grass. Yet they must realize they are not to mix blood with the aristocrats."[7] Fox's mountain heroes are always drawn with sympathy, and never does he let the reader forget their pride. If the bluegrass aristocrats are not to mix blood with the mountaineers, the mountaineers know their destiny lies in their own endeavors and not in any assistance that marriage with low-country gentry might bring them.

Minor figures also occasionally catch the reader's interest. Old Jason Hawn, young Jason's grandfather, is one of the lovable old persons that Fox frequently could draw. He is as genuine a mountaineer as ever breathed in fiction. One of the high points of the novel comes when old Jason hides his fleeing grandson from pursuing lawmen after the assassination of the "great man" at the state capital, then decides to turn him over to the law after he finds out what young Jason is accused of, but changes his mind again when he learns that a hundred thousand dollar reward has been offered for the capture and conviction of the murderer: "For a mule, a Winchester, and a hundred dollars I can git most any man in this country killed. Fer a thousand I reckon I could git hit proved that I had stole a side o' bacon or a hoss. Fer a hundred thousand I could git hit proved that the President of these United States killed that feller—an human natur' is about the same, I reckon, ever'whar. You don't git no grandson o' mine when thar's a bunch o' greenbacks like that tied to the rope that's a'pinin' to hang him."[8]

The old circuit rider, Uncle Lige, and his wife are also authentic, though they have only very minor roles in the novel. And there is a school teacher again, John Burnham by name, who may have been derived from Fox's image of himself. Some of the figures at the university in the bluegrass are drawn from Fox's recollections of his years at Kentucky University (Transylvania). St. Hilda, a bluegrass belle who has gone into the mountains to develop a school and who gives aid and training to young Jason when he first decides to prepare to compete in the outside world, is a woman of dedication and vision whose limited role is drawn from life.

But the plot is one of the more maudlin that Fox wrote. There are few if any surprises in it, and the sentiment is so contrived as to repel today's reader. There is always a quality about Fox's plots that suggests a lack of imagination. He was a better sketcher than a narrator. His stories lag and are so painfully clear that they often fail to stir the modern reader. In *The Heart of the Hills* the plot is again too obvious. No doubt, this lack of a suspenseful story line detracted from the book's appeal to the reading public in 1913 and accounted for Fox's failure to achieve with it another first-rate success.

Furthermore, there is repetition of theme in the story. Here again is the mountain waif—or waifs, in this case—hurled into the alien community of the valley bluegrass aristocrat. Displaying his best qualities, he overcomes all the handicaps he is born to and demonstrates clearly the native goodness of stock of the mountain folk. Be it Chad Buford, June Tolliver, or Jason Hawn, however, the story is clear. The ways of the old mountaineer are passing, but the destiny of the mountain young remains in the land of their fathers. Only Chad Buford heads for the West at the end of *The Little Shepherd*. But even Chad is bound to return, Fox suggests.

Reviews of *The Heart of the Hills* were mixed but somewhat querulous. In a very short review, the *Review of Reviews* noted that readers of Fox's earlier work would not be disappointed in his latest. "Three things can be said of all Mr. Fox's novels: They are strong; they are clean; they are never dull."[9] Such commentary suggested the genteel rationale behind all of Fox's writing that kept him abreast of the popular reading tastes but prevented him from advancing to the ranks of the first-rate fiction writers. Fox's books were strong in all of the tenets of Genteel Romanticism in an age when the best fiction writers had long since turned to Realism or Naturalism. But that the Fox books were never dull to the great average mind was abundantly clear; sales proved this.

The *Outlook,* too, was noteworthy for its praise. It found *The Heart of the Hills* "head and shoulders above the average novel of the season." *Outlook* noted that the book was semihistorical and of realistic intention in dealing with the Goebel murder and the "Tobacco War" but found that portion of the novel the least satisfactory: "Mr. Fox is supremely good where he always has been, in depicting the mountain folk and the mountain country of Kentucky; his boy and girl in the opening chapters are worth ten books about industrial and political events."[10] The *Literary Digest* was happy to note that Fox was continuing to write with such sincerity and appreciation of the mountain folk who are "striving to hold their own against a pressure of civilization they do not comprehend."[11]

Probably the most significant praise for the book came, however, from Frederic T. Cooper in *Bookman.* Cooper, who had not always been noted as a Fox enthusiast, said he had failed to give Fox his due in the past because he, Cooper, was not interested in the "ignorant, vindictive, half-savage natives of the Cumberland Mountains." But, disregarding the setting and types about which he wrote, "Mr. Fox is one of the few true artists among the younger makers of American fiction. His people are not characters in a book; they are living actualities. His background is not a picturesque stage setting; it is a section of the country he knows best, torn bodily from its mountain fastnesses and flung before us in all its primitive ruggedness." Cooper noted that Fox had successfully combined the local color with themes that were not local "but as wide as humanity itself."[12]

Other reviewers were, however, more guarded. The *Independent* found a contradiction or contrast between the truthful, realistic aspects of the story and the artificial or romantic:

He gives us an exact and vivid idea of the life of the Kentucky mountaineers and does the same for the Blue Grass Kentuckians. But then, after having gone so far and so successfully into truth, he turns about and places his four main characters . . . in such a highly colored, strained and unnatural relationship to each other that he throws his whole book out of focus and the reader involuntarily repudiates some of the most significant features of the novel. In the midst of simplicity Mr. Fox has placed artificiality and it is a very evident misfit.

The *Independent* also noted mechanical handicaps—tautology, involved sentences, grandiose language, and faulty chronology in the growth of the four main characters. But the descriptions, said the reviewer, were good: "There is nothing artificial about them and they are as refreshing as one of the mountain streams. Quite as perfect in their way as certain situations in the book which, considered separately from the story, are splendid pieces of dramatic action." The *Independent* found the work generally satisfactory if one recognized that Romance was an "autocrat" that frequently led its authors into pitfalls that blindfolded truth.[13]

Whereas the *Outlook* had disliked the semihistorical portions of the tale, the *Nation* found that the novel "leaves a clearer impression of contemporary history than of personal drama."[14] The book was an interesting social record and a vivid portrait of Kentucky in the last years of the nineteenth century. But the *Nation's* political proclivities may have suggested its decided interest in the social and economic features of the book, whereas the *Outlook* tended generally to shun such aspects of novel writing in 1913.

Both the *Dial* and the New York *Times* found the novel inferior even to Fox's own earlier work. "Mr. Fox seems to be only at his second best in this book, which means, no doubt, that he has worked out his richest veins and has to fall back upon toilings. The story would be striking enough if we were not all the time forced to contrast it with its predecessors," said W. M. Payne in the *Dial*. Even the feud between the Hawns and Honeycutts, Payne thought, was not clear; and the relationships of the two families were so confused that the reader had difficulty telling which was which, a criticism, incidentally, wholly justified by repeated readings.[15] The New York *Times* was even harsher in its findings; to it, Fox had no gifts for historical fiction: "Nor does a disposition to moralize and rhapsodize about the virtues and short-comings of the Kentuckians very much assist the general effect. At best in the present case we have only the reproduction of something we have been made familiar with. Yet the streak of poetry in Mr. Fox's fiction, and his incurably romantic point of view, are likely to keep him in favor with a class of readers which is by no means small."[16]

The note of annoyance in the *Times'* reaction no doubt represented that of the more important reviewers of the day who generally kept a discreet silence about Fox's latest production. *The Heart of the Hills* was, of course, widely read; but it failed to match Fox's earlier work in sales or in reader reaction. His veins had been worked, as the *Dial* noted; there was repetition in the mountain tale, and local color was past its prime. Fifty or twenty-five years earlier the book would have aroused greater interest. As it was, the novel did little more than sum up a small segment of one state's history and add another touch to the canvas Fox had already painted of the Cumberland Mountain area.

CHAPTER 9

Later Fiction and Decline

I In Happy Valley

F OX'S writing deteriorated in quality and decreased in quantity after the publication of *The Heart of the Hills*. Following the termination of his turbulent relationship with Fritzi in February, 1913, other problems peripheral to his life as a celebrated novelist intruded to prevent sustained literary effort. When a popular song using the title of *The Trail of the Lonesome Pine* was published in 1912, Fox was forced to bring suit to gain any financial return for the use of his title; and arrangements for drama and movie versions of his two most popular books also proved troublesome and time-consuming. He signed a drama contract for *The Little Shepherd of Kingdom Come* in the summer of 1913, but the play version was not forthcoming until 1916. The play writing had been first entrusted to Abraham Erlanger whose procrastinations over production caused Fox considerable annoyance during 1913 and 1914 until finally the play was placed with Eugene Walter.

As noted earlier, *The Trail of the Lonesome Pine* was eminently successful on the stage from the time of its first production until the 1920's. Cinema versions, however, proved more difficult. Fox carried on extensive negotiations between 1912 and 1916 for the filming of his story. Finally, when *The Trail* was released in 1916, it was not at all to Fox's liking. After his death, successful motion pictures were made of *The Trail* in 1922 and 1936. But, while he lived, his attempts to work with the film industry were more frustrating than satisfying. As for the movie rights to *The Little Shepherd of Kingdom Come,* he negotiated with Edward Hemmer in 1915 for a picture version that would star Jack Pickford, who had appeared earlier in *Tom Sawyer, Seventeen*, and *Freckles*. Actually, however, the only successful cinema version of *The Little Shepherd* came in 1928—once again, after his death.

In truth, Fox never found writing an easy assignment, and he was inclined to creative procrastination through much of his life. This characteristic was especially apparent when alternatives to writing were plentiful—and plentiful they were as Fox's financial security brought increased leisure and opportunities for recreation. Around Big Stone Gap, he hunted, fished, and often walked alone through the hills. He enjoyed golf and frequently played with his close friend Bascom Slemp, local political tyro and future secretary to President Calvin Coolidge. Amidst the many problems of the play and movie versions of his two most successful books, Fox found time to enjoy extensive vacations at resort areas in this country. Hunting trips to Idaho and Wyoming, fishing excursions off the South Carolina coast, winters in Florida, and summers along the coast of Maine at Bar Harbor occupied his time and energies.[1] The Adirondack Mountains of New York state were another favorite haunt where he often visited. In 1914 he made his first trip abroad. He dined with the Duke and Dutchess of Sutherland while in England, hobnobbed with other nobility, and enjoyed fox hunting and riding to the hounds in the English fashion. At least one more time before his death in 1919, he journeyed in England and on the Continent. With the money and friends needed for such excursions, Fox increased considerably his leisure time activities in the last years of his life—always to the neglect of his literary endeavors.

By March, 1917, however, he was back at Big Stone Gap on a more permanent basis. When the United States entered World War I, Fox volunteered for active duty but was refused on account of his poor health. He did speak on War Bond and Red Cross drives and signed up in the summer of 1918 to go overseas to read his stories to the troops, but the war ended before he got across. Meanwhile, *Scribner's Magazine* brought out another series of mountain stories in monthly issues from January to October, 1917. In the fall of that year they were published in a book entitled *In Happy Valley.*

The *Happy Valley* stories center around the inhabitants of a particularly isolated section in Kentucky between Black Mountain and Pine Mountain. The same characters frequent several of the stories, but the plots are all separate and distinct; indeed, the story lines are thin. *In Happy Valley* might more properly be called a series of descriptive sketches or vignettes of mountain life. Types appearing in his earlier works—even some of the same names—are to be found here. There is the school teacher, St. Hilda, who has established a mission school in the valley; another school-teacher friend from Virginia assists. And there is a doctor who administers to the needs of the mountain community much as one of Fox's friends had done in an earlier day. Characters such as Pleasant Trouble, Ira Combs, Lum Chapman, Juno Camp, Jeb Mullins, and the girl "Allaphair" illustrate Fox's view of the best mountain types. Outsiders— such as Mary Holden (the Virginia school teacher), the young doctor on Lonesome Creek, and Professor James Blagden of New England—come into the mountains and find a stimulating and pleasant locale in which to work. They also learn the fine qualities of the outwardly uncouth and unsophisticated mountaineers. Exposure to the isolated realm of the mountaineers generally converts these outsiders; and, like Jack Hale in *The Trail of the Lonesome Pine,* they decide to remain for a lifetime in the Cumberlands.

"The Courtship of Allaphair" reveals a prideful mountain girl who will accept courtship from no one. Finally, she succumbs to the school teacher, Iry Combs, who is himself mountain born but has been to the bluegrass to school. His polish and knowledgable ways at first irritate the mountain girl; but, when it comes to a contest for her affections between Jay Dawn and Combs, she places her heart with the teacher. In a fight with proper boxing rules, "no wrasslin', no bitin', no gougin'," Combs manages to defeat his opponent and to win the hand of the independent Allaphair. The girl's disdain for her many would-be suitors and her boyish manners set her apart from the traditional picture of the mountain woman's subservience in a man's world.

"The Compact of Christopher" and "The Angel from Viper" are two of the best sketches in the book because they concern children, a type of story, as noted, that Fox was always most adept at recounting. Christopher, a mountain lad who is attending St. Hilda's mission school, has a habit of dropping by Jeb Mullins' still on numerous occasions. A particular "new Christmas" visit rouses the ire of the tender-hearted St. Hilda who can't whip her pupil, but she vows that Christopher's mother will have to do it. The story ends poignantly when Christopher agrees to stop drinking if his mother will, and St. Hilda realizes that Christopher's main problem is not visitation at the still but the home environment that engenders it.

"The Angel from Viper" is about a lovable ten-year-old mountain tyke with a fondness for stretching the truth. The angel, Willie, brings his younger brother James Henry to the mission school. After accusing "Jeems Henery" of being the "gamblin'est, lyin'est, cussin'est" boy on Viper Creek, Willie finally admits his own possession of these distinctions. But he has helped reform some of the other mountain boys, and St. Hilda in her characteristic compassion is unable to punish the lad.

"The Lord's Own Level" notes how Lum Chapman, the blacksmith, can find a coal vein easier than the geologists by employing his own homespun engineering techniques. It also records Lum's love affair with a girl already pregnant by a married man. Fox explains that "there were peculiar customs in Happy Valley, due to the [circuit] 'rider's' long absences, so that sometimes a baby might without shame be present at the wedding of its own parents."[2] Lum takes the girl in, and without a formal proposal she turns to his housekeeping with the tacit understanding that "the circuit-rider'll be 'roun' two weeks from next Sunday."[3]

"The Marguise of Queensberry" explains how Miss Mary Holden of Virginia teaches the proper rules of boxing to two mountain toughs who, unknown to her, are quarreling over her affections. After teaching the lesson, she leaves them to ponder their fate as she departs from the valley with her true lover. "The Last Christmas Gift" reveals how a hard mountaineer, shot by his own wife, takes the secret of his assassin to his grave as a last Christmas gift to her.

"The Pope of the Big Sandy" is a man of the mountains who has made his way in the world to an affluent position on Park Avenue in New York. He is visited on his deathbed by the Judge of Happy Valley who learns, when he comes to the city, that his old friend has bequeathed his money to the inhabitants of Happy Valley and to the children of the woman the Pope once loved, Sally Ann Spurlock. Having made his money from the coal in the hills, the Pope wishes to extend his philanthropy after his death. The bequest is made more moving by the failure of the Pope to win the one office he has coveted, that of city councilman

in his home town, and more ironical by the fact of his defeat
by Bill Maddox, the man who married his earlier sweetheart,
Sally Ann.

In "The Goddess of Happy Valley," the longest sketch in the
collection, Professor James Blagden of New England falls in love
with Juno Camp, a girl of the mountains, while she is studying
at his school in the North. When Juno marries him, she extracts
a promise that he not visit her home or her people for five years.
Later, when typhoid fever breaks out in Juno's home, Happy
Valley, she returns to aid her old friends and neighbors; and,
when she succumbs to the illness herself, her husband breaks
his promise and comes to the Southern mountain regions to care
for her. At first, he is appalled at the dirt and ignorance of his
wife's people; but he quickly realizes the need and his opportunity. He takes up his wife's position as visiting nurse in the
mountain cabins and soon is hailed as "Doctor Jim." Juno re-
covers, but complications develop when one of her former lovers
returns to kill the doctor. The mountain people protect "Juno's
man," and the professor finally wins over his erstwhile enemy by
helping him to find a job and straighten out his twisted life. The
story is again one of the awakening of an outsider to the worth
and goodness of the isolated mountain folk. The professor leaves
the area with the pledge that he will help raise money for the
mission. "I don't know where any more good is being done, and
I don't know any people who are more worth being helped
than—your people," he tells his wife.[4]

"The Battle-Prayer of Parson Small" recounts the efforts of the
parson to turn Jeb Mullins from his moonshining ways. Jeb
challenges the parson to a fight after a chastisement in church;
the parson accepts but, just before the contest, utters a prayer
in Mullins' presence recounting his own mighty exploits with the
knife: "O Lawd, thou knowest that I visit my fellow man with
violence only with thy favor and in thy name. Thou knowest that
when I laid Jim Thompson an' Si Marcum in thar graves it was
by thy aid. Thou knowest how I disembowelled with my trusty
knife the miserable sinner Hank Smith....An' hyeh's another
who meddles with thy servant and profanes thy day. I know this
hyeh Jeb Mullins is offensive in thy sight an' fergive me, O Lawd,
but I'm a-goin' to cut his gizzard plum' out."[5] Such language has
the desired effect: Mullins flees and forgets the challenge. Later,
when Mullins destroys his still and is converted at meeting, the

parson feels he has made a conquest for God; but the reader learns at the very end that Mullins has destroyed his old still only because a newly purchased one is to be installed the next week.

"The Christmas Tree on Pigeon" relates the efforts of a doctor to keep a Christmas tree he has installed in the schoolhouse for the Pigeon Creek folk from being destroyed by raiders from across the mountain. Viewing the Christmas tree as an innovation of distrusted outsiders, the raiders have earlier destroyed the one tree that the mountain community has known. This time, however, they are thwarted by the doctor who organizes a posse to protect the tree. The doctor of this story is the lover of Mary Holden, the teacher of the "Marquise of Queensberry" sketch; and "Christmas Tree on Pigeon" ends with the marriage of these two "fotched-on" people who have come into the hills to aid a folk they have learned to respect and love.

The ten stories of *In Happy Valley* do not show Fox in any new literary light, and they further advance the thought that he was quickly exhausting the one source of his storytelling fame. Furthermore, that source was beginning to lose its fascination for many American readers; the vogue of the mountaineer tale was about eclipsed. Reviews of *In Happy Valley* in 1917 and 1918 hinted this fact. The *Dial* noted that the mountains and mountaineers were not as isolated as they once were and that "the inspiration that he [Fox] seemed to draw from those earlier days at the Gap, when the mountains were really what one imagines the mountains to be, is somewhat dimmed, just as the mountain character has acquired a veneer of outer-worldliness." Yet the *Dial* also said that Fox was still able to see beneath the surface of his characters and was able "to enrich mere incident with the warmth that comes from an appreciation of the values from which it springs."[6]

H. W. Boynton in *Bookman* found the *Happy Valley* stories good and "affecting," although "less true to life than to that wistful dream of life which is called sentiment."[7] The *New Republic* stated that Fox still knew how to capture primitive instincts and passions of the impoverished inhabitants of his valleys. To the reviewer, the stories were concerned with real people whom Fox had succeeded in making lovable to his readers.[8] E. P. Wyckoff felt that reading the stories was "like

greeting old friends, not like being bored by tiresome acquaintances."⁹

The stories are, indeed, like old friends. They repeat the
settings, character types, and themes of Fox's earliest writings,
though there is a softer touch of civilization sensed in the sketches.
Life is not quite so harsh or so rugged as it is in the *Hell-fer-
Sartain* or in the *Blue-grass and Rhododendron* volumes. The
passage of the years had brought some changes to the mountain
world. Mission teachers, typhoid control, and Christmas trees had
come to the hills and valleys of the Cumberland. In recording the
more recent phases of mountain life, however, Fox degenerated
further into the sentiment that had marred his writing from the
beginning—and at a time when the reading public was less inclined to tolerate it. *In Happy Valley* did not fare well with a
public moving from early twentieth-century surety into the rigors
and realities of World War I.

II *The Historical Novel*

At the same time that it was apparent Fox would need to
find a new voice to regain his earlier audiences, he continued to
find it increasingly difficult to maintain his writing regimen.
Always he had to return to the family home at Big Stone Gap
to do much writing; yet more and more he had turned to the
salons of New York and of the world away from the Gap for
the relaxation and amusement that his nature demanded. Having
worn his subject thin, he was not personally prepared to write as
consistently as before. His earlier stories had been completed in
fairly short periods; his later works frequently took two or three
years. Between *The Trail of the Lonesome Pine* and *The Heart
of the Hills* five years elapsed. It was another four years before
his next book, *In Happy Valley*, appeared.¹⁰

Nevertheless, during his last months, John Fox sought earnestly
to leave the world another effort that he hoped would be his
masterpiece, his classic. Abandoning contemporary mountain lore,
perhaps recognizing its depletion as a fictional subject, he turned
to the history of Kentucky and Virginia for a new work. It was
a historical novel, and he spent considerable time researching
and checking his facts for the effort. He used his own family
history as inspiration and source for much of the material. With
no book that he ever wrote did Fox struggle more; for none, did
he have higher hopes. Still unfinished at the time of his death

(only the last chapter remained to be written), it was completed by his sister and published in the fall of 1920.[11]

Erskine Dale—Pioneer is a novel of the American Revolution and of the American Indian. The book opens dramatically in the heart of the Kentucky "bloody land" where an Indian boy, "White Arrow," has sought refuge at the gate of a pioneer fort during an Indian attack. The boy turns out to be a white lad who has been brought up by the Indians after he and his mother were captured years before. The boy's father, a Virginia fron-tiersman-explorer of the Kentucky realm, appears at the fort with help in time to save the pioneers. But he is mortally wounded as he enters the gate during his daring rescue, and he lives only long enough to reveal that the mysterious "White Arrow" is really his son, whom he had thought lost years before. The boy is, indeed, Erskine Dale, heir to one of the rich landed estates in the Tide-water of Virginia. And when his heritage is discovered, he is soon sent to the East by his Kentucky friends to learn refined ways and to meet his relatives.

The book constantly shifts from the cultured atmosphere of Virginia and Williamsburg to the Western wilderness area of the Indians and pioneers. The next chapters reveal Erskine's intro-duction to his Tidewater heritage. His uncle warmly receives him and points out that Red Oaks plantation is really his as the son of the eldest heir, now dead in Kentucky. There is a beautiful cousin, Barbara Dale, who promptly captures Erskine's heart, though he learns that he has a rival in Dane Grey, a snobbish aristocrat who scorns Erskine as an uncouth child of the wilder-ness.

All the elements for popular romance are at hand: the poor but gallant and basically well-bred hero; the charming, coquettish heroine; and the insufferable, treacherous villain. Dane Grey is a traitor; he works behind patriot lines to acquire Indian support for the British during the war for independence; he is found out and slain only at the end—in both cases by Erskine, of course. Barbara, who has never quite succumbed to some of Erskine's wilderness manners, learns the truth finally and goes with her hero back to the Kentucky frontier to make a home with him in the new land of the West.

How this romance is worked out during the course of the American Revolution is of less interest, however, than the re-lationship with the Indians that Erskine maintains. A foster child of Kahtoo, an old Indian chieftain of the Shawnees, Erskine still feels an obligation to the Indians who reared him. When asked to return to the tribal home by Kahtoo, he feels this tie. Fox makes much of Erskine as a connecting link between the savages and the white man and between the Tidewater aristocrats and the wilderness pioneers. At times, Erskine considers the incongruity between the two worlds he inhabits. He cannot shirk his white man's role, nor can he completely abandon his Indian upbringing. During a pagan dance in the camp of the Shawnee, "his thoughts went backward to his friends at the fort and on back to the big house on the James, to Harry and Hugh—and Barbara; and he wondered what they would think if they could see him there; could see the gluttonous feast and those naked savages stamping around the fire with barbaric grunts and cries to the thumping of a drum. Where did he belong?"[12]

Erskine has fled his Indian home, not because of an essential lack of sympathy with the Indian's way of life, but because of the ill treatment he has received from one member of the tribe, Crooked Lightning, a brave older than he. Why the foster son of a chieftain would have to put up with such harassment is not made clear, for certainly Erksine's position with Kahtoo is firmly established and he is treated as the heir apparent to the old leader's role. Fox, who needed some excuse to get his hero back into the stream of white life, chose a rather clumsy expedient for doing it.

At any rate, Erskine early makes a trip back to the Indian territory at the request of his foster father who fears his own time is not long on this earth and who wants his foster son to intervene to prevent an alliance between the Shawnee and the British. Kahtoo fears such an alliance bodes ill for the Indians, and Erskine is quick to agree. Erskine makes a futile attempt to dissuade the Indians from their British connection at a council meeting where he encounters the treacherous Dane Grey working surreptitiously for an opposite purpose. He also finds a white woman and her part Indian daughter in the camp of Kahtoo. The mysterious woman eventually turns out to be his mother—Kahtoo had purchased her from wandering tribesmen—and the lovely Early Morn is, therefore, his half-sister. Until he discovers her identity, there is some indication that Erskine is tempted to forget Barbara Dale and marry into the tribe. As it is, Erskine's interest in the Indian girl is just enough to cause Dane Grey to

take word back to Barbara; and, until she learns the true relationship of the two, Barbara shuns Erskine as a prospective
suitor.

During the course of the Revolution, the Indians attack the
Kentucky outposts and Erskine returns again to the Indian lands—
this time with George Rogers Clark on a punitive expedition.
Kahtoo, the white woman, Early Morn, and others of the tribe
are saved from the vengeance of Clark when Erskine intercedes.
The wicked Shawnee, however, are dispersed; their homes
burned; their crops destroyed. It is during this military venture
that Erskine learns that the white woman is really his mother.
But she cannot be persuaded to go back to white civilization;
her life is now too much committed to the Indians. As for
Early Morn, she becomes the squaw of an earlier rival of Erskine
among the Indians.

The Indian portions of the story, occupying much of the latter
half of the book, are better done than the Kentucky and Virginia
scenes. Fox's penchant for sentimentality is not given so free a
hand here, and the sketchiness of the portraits in the book generally seems less out of place when he is writing of Indian
characters than when dealing with whites. Fox effectively depicts
the conflicts in young Dale's mind as he contemplates the choice
he must make of remaining as Kahtoo's heir with the Shawnee
tribe to take over the chieftainship or of returning to the white
man's world and his inheritance on the James. In taking the
middle way, he chooses the white man's wilderness; Kentucky
will be his home.

On the whole, however, the plot of *Erskine Dale—Pioneer*
is too sketchily drawn to be very moving, and the characters
are too vaguely portrayed to be convincing. The story moves so
rapidly that Fox takes the reader through a period of over
fifteen years in about two hundred and fifty pages. His narrative,
actually the most involved of any he ever wrote, is only outlined,
shadowed, hinted—not explicitly woven. This sketchiness gives
the impression of a hastily written book—though, in truth, it was
several months in the making—and of a lack of finesse in construction. In addition, the plot, though lacking in detail, has
few surprises. One knows the role of each character when he is
first introduced and the denouement of each incident when it
is projected.

Moreover, there are no social mores or mountain customs to

relieve the novel this time. Historically, it is accurate enough—there are numerous allusions to factual characters and incidents—but the story, for the most part, strains the credulity of the modern reader. Circumstance is everywhere; fate is too often benevolent. Some of the descriptions are apt—particularly the natural settings—but they are scarcely sufficient to redeem the book. It was unfortunate that, instead of writing the classic he dreamed of, Fox left the world as his last effort one of his poorest creations. Surely the suggestion is that he was written out by 1919 and would have been increasingly ill at ease in the literary world of the 1920's.

Reviewers were still often kind to Fox, however, when the novel appeared. They noted that the story had all the ingredients characteristic of popular fiction—two duels, a long-lost mother, a narrow escape from being burned at the stake, a wonderful black horse ("Firefly") and dashing horsemen, and the usual love affair. The *Outlook*, which referred to the "dash, fire and romance" of such stories, thought that the novel was "perhaps the very best of his many romances."[13] The New York *Times* indicated that the book had plenty of color and gave "an interesting picture of the period with which it deals." It found the figure of Erskine Dale, "the bluest of Virginia blue blood," appealing.[14]

Perhaps the *Catholic World* and *Cleveland* magazine best suggested, however, the future usefulness of the book. "It is a good book to give to the American boy," said the *World*, "for it abounds in stirring adventures, and at the same time gives a good insight into the everyday life of the pioneers."[15] "The dialog is full of 'go' and the book will appeal immensely to intermediates," said *Cleveland* magazine.[16] Obviously, this suggests *Erskine Dale's* only audience today. If used at all, the book should be placed before juveniles who may want a dashing story of the old Romantic school to record the history of the pioneer wilderness and the Revolutionary War days. That it could any longer interest adult readers, more sophisticated today than in 1920, seems hardly possible.

III   *Death and Burial*

Erskine Dale is not one of John Fox's better books, nor did it bring Fox the final acclaim he had hoped for. If it had come twenty years earlier, the novel might have succeeded with public and critics. But the turn-of-the-century fad for historical fiction had lost its momentum by 1920. It is ironic that the work Fox had hoped would launch him into a new field to insure his literary immortality is the least known of his books and the least worthy of our appreciation today. It adds not one iota to the sum-total of his literary position; instead of marking the climax of his career, it represents the final sputtering-out of a literary life that was on the decline from 1908 onward.

As it turned out, Fox was to have no chance to move in the new directions *Erskine Dale* suggests. Whether additional years would have brought a more solid literary accomplishment, no one will ever know. On July 8, 1919, at the age of fifty-six, he died of pneumonia contracted only a few days earlier while on a walking and fishing trip through the mountain country around Norton, Virginia, near Big Stone Gap. His illness was sudden; his death unexpected. Only a few nights before he died, he had attended a hill-country carnival and had enlivened the evening with his own singing, playing, and dancing to the old mountain tunes he knew so well. Burial was in the family plot at Paris, Kentucky, near where he was born. Thus, he was carried—to quote his own words on another, similar occasion—"from dreams of green hills, gray walls, sharp peaks and clear, swift water over the Wilderness Road to the rolling sweep of green slopes, from wood thrush to meadow lark, from rhododendron to blue grass, from mountain to lowland, and left in the beautiful blue grass country he loved so well."[17]

CHAPTER 10

The Residue

A LTHOUGH Thomas Nelson Page could write in 1919 of the "undeniable art stamped on every volume" Fox wrote and of "the gift of the masters" that the author possessed, and although sales of his books attest to the Kentuckian's immense popularity in his own day, John Fox, Jr., is little more than a footnote in American literary history today.[1] Whether this placement is just or unjust only future readers and critics and, more particularly, the passage of time can vouchsafe. Certainly this study of his work suggests its extreme sentimentality, its tendentious morality, its contrived plots, and its mediocre character study. That Fox is destined for a very high place in the literary future seems extremely doubtful. But the footnote does remain, and the residue of worth from his abundant materials must be delineated.

I *Style and Technique*

In manner, Fox's books and stories give him only the most tenuous claim to literary notice. There is no evidence that he ever theorized about the writing of fiction. He seldom said anything about the technical aspects of his own work. For the most part, he shunned literary conclaves and did not seek to number writers among his friends.[2] Rather, he knew lawyers, engineers, businessmen, actors, musicians, and talented *bons vivants* that the accidents of environment or interest threw him among. He was a story teller, an extoller of Kentucky, a chronicler of the Cumberlands—uninterested in or oblivious to the niceties of fictional theorizing. In technique and style, he simply conformed to the age of which he was a part.

The 1890's and the first years of the twentieth century was a nostalgic period of innocence when feeling was dominant in American reading taste. James Whitcomb Riley, Will Carleton.

and Eugene Field were among the most popular poets of the day. Fictional interest ran to such favorites as Gene Stratton Porter, Harold Bell Wright, Kate Douglas Wiggin, and the American Winston Churchill. The demand was for sentiment, simple, strong, and tearful. An easy optimism and sentimentality were in the air. Fox, naturally inclined by temperament toward the Romantic view of life, fitted easily into the tendency of his times without attempting to blaze literary trails by experimenting with new techniques in writing.

Fox's worst literary faults, therefore, are those generally characteristic of the popular writing of his era. In his longer works especially, his propensity is for Victorian gentility. His friend Thomas Nelson Page noted "not one foul line, not one salacious suggestion, not one ignoble thought" in all Fox's writing.[3] The remoteness of Fox from any semblance of the Naturalism of the 1890's might be surmised from Page's comment. Although in his better short stories he sometimes revealed characteristics of a mild Realism, Fox was basically and invariably an inveterate Romantic in his novels. The popular theme of an unequal love match—so characteristic of the fiction of his day—he exploits time and again. Like the popular reader of his times, and like the Southern gallant Fox was, he is drawn to beauty and heroism. The noble, good, heroic principal characters, male or female— especially the bluegrass types—are lifeless and stereotyped. Plots of coincidence and hackneyed similarity make his narratives seem antiquated and musty today. Nothing about the manner or technique of writing in them suggests a literary merit that will ever establish them in the annals of American classics.

Nevertheless, a liberal education in Greek and Latin led Fox to a sense of form and order, simplicity, and directness in his fiction that is most marked in his best work, the short stories. Like most of the local colorists, he failed at the novel. But in his better short stories—perhaps half a dozen out of about forty-five he wrote—he sketches a scene, suggests a character, or sets a mood that marks the competent hand of a skilled craftsman. At his best, he could equal Bret Harte, George Washington Cable, or his fellow chronicler of the Southern Appalachians, Mary Noailles Murfree.[4] Indeed, in clarity and sense of immediacy Fox often surpasses Murfree in the mountaineer story. William Dean Howells noted in a comparison of the two authors that "Mr. Fox has the formidable priority of Miss Murfree in her stories of kindred nature and human nature. It should therefore be all the more gratifying to him if the reader recognizes a fresh vision in his way of seeing them, and a novel touch in his way of presenting them. Both vision and touch, without being surer, perhaps, are clearer and more direct." Howells attributed this to the fact that Fox had arrived later than Murfree when the right methods of fiction had been ascertained: "He has not had to outlive the false school in which we of another generation were bred, and whose influence Miss Murfree did not escape."[5] In this one respect, at least, Fox may have profited from being one of the last of the local-color group.

Fox loved nature and painted it well. Like Jason Hawn in *The Heart of the Hills,* or like his own father, Fox knew all the flowers, plants, bushes, birds, animals, and fish life of the Cumberlands. Depicting nature always as a source of comfort to man, he was drawn to Keats, most sensuous of the Romantics, as an early favorite. He had a reticent note of dry humor, too, that occasionally sparks his best sketches. Like the mountaineer, however, he most often combined humor with pathos. He employed dialect judiciously—never overdoing it as the worst local colorists frequently did. And, as John Patterson noted in the *Library of Southern Literature,* Fox possessed in a marked degree "the high literary quality, like Meredith or Stevenson, of giving a single significant detail which will light up a character instantaneously."[6] No better brief sketches than "On Hell-fer-Sartain Creek," "Courtin' on Cutshin," "Preaching on Kingdom-Come," "The Passing of Abraham Shivers," or "A Purple Rhododendron" exist in the regional literature of American local color.

II *Subjects*

a. THE BORDER AREA. It is because of the matter of his writing—his subjects—rather than the manner, however, that Fox has some importance today. To begin with, he made a valuable contribution to literary history by recording the tensions of the border-state area in the Civil War time. Civil War fiction was well established by 1900, but Fox's principal contribution to the genre in *The Little Shepherd of Kingdom Come* was the first novel to treat the border area of Kentucky with any degree of authenticity. In the boy Chad Buford, Fox displays the conflicts between loyalty to the Union and sentimental and family attachments to the Confederacy that marked the torment of many a middle and eastern Kentucky family in 1860. As we have noted, the mountain people were largely for the flag; they had known no other attachment since Revolutionary War days. And in their backward state of development, they still maintained feelings of intense Americanism that had been aroused by the struggle with Britain for independence. In addition, they had few associations with the landed or slaveholding classes of the rest of the South. The few who did own slaves often went with the Confederacy. (Note the Turners in *The Little Shepherd*.) But such people were in the minority in the mountains. Indeed, the Union sentiment of the Appalachian region—including eastern Kentucky—was a decisive factor in the war. According to Fox:

The American mountaineer was discovered . . . at the beginning of the war, when the Confederate leaders were counting on the presumption that Mason and Dixon's Line was the dividing line between the North and South, and formed, therefore, the plan of marching an army from Wheeling, in West Virginia, to some point on the lakes, and thus dissevering the North at one blow. The plan seemed so feasible that it is said to have materially aided the sale of Confederate bonds in England, but when Captain Garnett, a West Point graduate, started to carry it out, he got no farther than Harper's Ferry. When he struck the mountains, he struck enemies who shot at his men from ambush, cut down bridges before him, carried the news of his march to the Federals, and Garnett himself fell with a bullet from a mountaineer's squirrel rifle at Harper's Ferry. Then the South began to realize what a long, lean, powerful arm of the Union it was that the Southern mountaineer stretched through its very vitals; for that arm helped hold Kentucky in the Union by giving preponderance to the Union sympathizers in the Bluegrass; it kept the East Tennesseans loyal to the man; it made West Virginia, as the phrase goes, "secede from secession"; it drew out a horde of one hundred thousand volunteers, when Lincoln called for troops, depleting Jackson County, Kentucky, for instance, of every male under sixty years of age and over fifteen, and it raised a hostile barrier between the armies of the coast and the armies of the Mississippi. The North has never realized, perhaps, what it owes for its victory to this non-slaveholding Southern mountaineer.[7]

Perhaps no other work of American fiction so justly presents the Civil War loyalties of these mountain people as does *The Little Shepherd of Kingdom Come.*

Furthermore, the family conflicts in the bluegrass are amply

illustrated in the novel. The division within the Dean family—
one son going with the Union, the other with the South—is
suggestive of the terrible trial many a family of that border
area endured during the war. Also, the portrait of Brutus Dean,
the Abolitionist uncle of the Dean family, a portrait suggested
by Cassius M. Clay, further illustrates the family divisions of the
time. Though the bluegrass was Southern in sentiment and
kinship, and prided itself on many aspects of ante bellum Southern
society, traditional ties of union with the nation were also strong.
Frequently internal family conflict separating members from each
other and internal conflict within the individual himself were the
results. Fictionally, Fox records these family ordeals as no other
novelist before or since has done.

b. CONTRASTING KENTUCKY WORLDS: BLUEGRASS AND MOUN-
TAIN. Fox also demonstrated in his stories and novels the fictional possibilities of contrasting regional types in a single state.
He chose Kentucky as his locale because he knew it, but he also
chose it because he loved the land. Just a few years earlier, his
friend James Lane Allen had written of the bluegrass. Other
writers had touched on the mountain people. But none before
Fox (and few since) had so carefully marked out the contrasting
characteristics of the people of both regions of that state. In at
least four novels (*The Kentuckians, The Little Shepherd of Kingdom Come, The Trail of the Lonesome Pine,* and *The Heart of
the Hills*), in one nonfictional book (*Blue-grass and Rhodo-
dendro*n), and in several short stories, Fox dwelt on characters
from both the bluegrass and the mountains and indicated their
distinctiveness.

Born in the bluegrass, returned to it at death, Fox regarded
this part of the state as only a native son could. Writing primarily
of the period from 1885 to 1900 (except for *The Little Shepherd
of Kingdom Come* which deals, of course, with the ante bellum
era), he painted the bluegrass type as a patrician. Founded on
ante bellum values of a class society, the bluegrass patrician world
was, however, gradually breaking up by the end of the nineteenth
century. The older code had been one of chivalry, honor, family
ties, beautiful women held on a pedestal, a social world of dancing, fox hunting, and mint juleps. Much of the aristocratic
tradition remained in the Fox novels. The Deans and Major
Buford of *The Little Shepherd* show that world before the

Civil War. The Pendletons of *The Heart of the Hills,* Marshall and Anne Bruce of *The Kentuckians,* and the numerous engineer-entrepreneur bluegrass types of the stories reveal that older society coming to grips in a later era with new economic facts of life.

As the old order passed, the bluegrass aristocrats had to adjust to a different world. When iron and coal were open for exploitation in the 1880's, many of them went to the mountains to recoup their fortunes or to restore their waning prestige. The Fox brothers themselves in their enterprises at Jellico and Big Stone Gap were a fair illustration of this endeavor. A certain decadence, illustrated fictionally in Marshall of *The Kentuckians* and in Crittenden in the novel of the same title, showed a tendency on the part of some to bemoan their fallen estate and to escape life in drinking and in irresponsibility. But they always found themselves again—whether it was in the Spanish-American War, as in the case of Crittenden, or in the new engineering feats in the mountains, as was the case with Gray Pendleton or John Hale. The basic nobility and chivalry of this type character who lived by a code, by a set of rules, are clearly established. When the patrician comes in contact with the mountain world, this distinction is made clear.

In the mountains, on the other hand, life knew fewer rules. The mountain characters in Fox's fiction are, if anything, independent of rigid rules or forms. They have their code—that of the feudsman, for example,—but it allows much greater independence of action—particularly in regard to the social forms—than does the bluegrass code. When the independent, plebian mountain man meets the patrician of the bluegrass, he is invariably puzzled by the world he encounters and eventually withdraws to his own realm of the mountains, though often the wiser for his contact. Boone Stallard of *The Kentuckians* finds an ideal in the bluegrass but recognizes his destiny is with his own kind in the hills. Jason and Mavis Hawn of *The Heart of the Hills* return to the mountains and to each other after their enticement by bluegrass manners and their flirtations with bluegrass lovers.

The mountaineers of the stories frequently are awakened to something finer in life when the outside engineers like Hale and teachers like St. Hilda come into their realm, but they never choose to leave their world in the final analysis. June Tolliver of *The Trail of the Lonesome Pine* seriously considers a break with her apparent destiny, but in the end she and her bluegrass engineer decide to remain in Lonesome Cove. Only Chad in *The Little Shepherd* makes the break, as he heads for the West at the end of the novel. But, as noted earlier, Chad has really been transformed from mountain type to bluegrass type through the course of the story. This transformation is not quite satisfactory, but it enables Fox to make one of his few exceptions to the principle of separate realms for each type of character.[8]

Generally, Fox's contrasts of the bluegrass and mountain people show basic strengths and weaknesses in each and suggest possibilities for cooperation in development of their state and region; but socially, the futures of the two seem forever divided in his mind: he seldom allows his characters from one area to remain permanently in the world of the other.

c. "OUR CONTEMPORARY ANCESTORS": MOUNTAIN LOCAL COLOR. By far, John Fox's greatest accomplishment in literature, however, was in his local-color portraits of the Cumberland mountaineers. He came late to the genre of regionalism, but he made a contribution not surpassed by many of his predecessors; indeed, in some cases his work is superior to theirs. In his lectures on the mountain people, Fox often referred to them as "our contemporary ancestors" because they lived so like the pioneer forefathers of the rest of the country.[9] This apt phrase suggests the modern interest in the Southern mountain region by sociologists, historians, and folklorists. From their origin and history to their customs, Fox wrote honestly of the mountaineers and left a legacy for future interpreters of Appalachia.

Although he recognized possible descendants of bond servants, redemptioners, "vicious runaway criminals and the trashiest of the poor whites" among the mountain folk, Fox thought the primary origin of the Kentucky mountaineers was in good Scotch-Irish stock.[10] He traced, particularly in *Blue-grass and Rhododendron,* the roots of the mountaineers back to North Carolina, South Carolina, and Virginia. Part of the pioneer band that came across Cumberland Gap in the 1780's and 1790's, these people remained in the mountain fastnesses probably through several quirks of luck, such as a broken latch-trace, or they were pushed to the hills by economic deprivation:

From 1720 to 1780, the settlers in southwest Virginia, middle North

Carolina and western South Carolina were chiefly Scotch and Scotch-Irish. They were active in the measures preceding the outbreak of the Revolution, and they declared independence at Abington, Va., even before they did at Mecklenburg, N. C. In these districts they were the largest element in the patriot army, and they were greatly impoverished by the war. Being too poor or too conscientious to own slaves, and unable to compete with them as the planter's field hand, blacksmith, carpenter, wheel-wright, and man-of-all-work, especially after the invention of the cotton-gin in 1792, they had no employment and were driven to mountain and sand-hill. . . . Among prominent mountain families direct testimony or unquestioned tradition point usually to Scotch-Irish ancestry, sometimes to pure Scotch origin, sometimes to English. Scotch-Irish family names in abundance speak for themselves, as do folk-words and folk-songs and the characteristics, mental, moral, and physical, of the people.[11]

Occasionally a patrician type of Virginia stock remained in the mountains, as did the ancestor of Chad Buford, the major's uncle in *The Little Shepherd of Kingdom Come,* who had been buried at Cumberland Gap after putting down family roots in that locale.

Fox granted, however, that Scotch-Irish thriftiness had decayed in the mountains: "The soil was poor; game was abundant; hunting bred idleness. There were no books, no schools, few church privileges, a poorly educated ministry, and the present illiteracy, thriftlessness, and poverty were easy results. Deedbooks show that the ancestors of men who now make their mark, often wrote a good hand."[12]

Yet, Fox was by no means unsympathetic in his portrait of the people. He had traveled among them and lived among them. He readily granted their hospitality, once the initial exchange had been made, their kindliness, honesty, loyalty, and their capabilities to learn when the opportunity was presented. Above all, they were patriotic, "Americans to the core," whose loyalties went back to the Revolution and, "imprisoned like a fossil in the hills," were never strained through the years that followed.[13] "To understand the mountaineer, you must go back to the Revolution," Fox wrote. "To do him justice you must give him the awful ordeal of a century of isolation and consequent ignorance in which to deteriorate. Do that and your wonder, perhaps, that he is so bad becomes a wonder that he is not worse."[14] The isolation and resulting ignorance in which he lived kept the mountaineer's society at near-Revolutionary War levels and contributed to the stalemated civilization that he knew: "Precisely for the same reason, the mountaineer's estimate of the value of human life, of the sanctity of the law, of a duty that overrides either—the duty of one blood kinsman to another—is the estimate of that day [1776] and not of this; and it is by the standards of that day and not of this that he is to be judged."[15]

The sum-total of Fox's writing provides a vast panorama of almost every facet of late nineteenth-century Cumberland Mountain life. The physical conditions of the landscape, the lack of adequate roads, the backward system of transportation, and the generally poor travel facilities are recorded along with the beauties and occasional harshness of the countryside and the abundance of the natural life. Economically, Fox shows the region as agricultural. Small crops of corn, sometimes fed to swine and livestock, sometimes turned into corn liquor in moonshining operations, provided a staple means of income. Moonshining, a source of money or barter for the mountaineer, meant economic livelihood. Hence, he considered it perfectly natural and correct to engage in the activity. Livestock in small numbers were also a means of existence. Some timbering took place in the fall, when logs were floated down the Kentucky River to the Frankfort market as the Turners did in *The Little Shepherd of Kingdom Come*.

As for education, schools and churches were rare. There were occasional one-room schools with a schoolmaster who "boarded around," as did Caleb Hazel in *The Little Shepherd*. "Blab schools," where the pupils studied aloud, reciting their lessons by rote, were common at one time; but such schools seldom lasted more than three months in the winter. Later, missionary-teachers from the outside, like St. Hilda in *The Heart of the Hills* and two of the *Happy Valley* sketches, sometimes established mission schools for the mountain youth. Endowed with good intelligence, many mountaineers could learn but had little opportunity. Once in a great while some of the younger people went to Transylvania University in the bluegrass to learn to preach or teach. Often the preacher, indeed, was the one source of formal knowledge for the isolated communities.

Medical services were as scattered as the educational opportunities. "Yarb doctors" such as the Red Fox of the mountains meagerly ministered to their neighbor's needs. The mountaineers knew next to nothing about sanitation. We recall that cholera took the foster parents of Chad in *The Little Shepherd*, "taking with it the breath of the unlucky and the unfit."[16] Scores died from typhoid fever epidemics spread by spring floods. Juno Camp, the goddess of Happy Valley, returned to her people from the North to aid in such an epidemic. "One cabin is built above another all the way up the creeks down there. The springs are by the stream. High water floods all of them, and the infection goes with the tide. And the poor things don't know— they don't know," she tells her husband, Professor Jim Blagden of New England.[17] In a memorable passage, Fox writes in the same story of the professor's stopping at a mountain cabin for midday dinner:

A slatternly woman with scraggling black hair, and with three dirty children clinging to her dirty apron, "reckoned she mought git him a bite," and disappeared. Flies swarmed over him when he sat in the porch. The rancid smell of bedding struck his sensitive nostrils from within. He heard the loud squawking of a chicken cease suddenly, and his hunger-gnawed stomach almost turned when he suddenly realized what it meant. When called within, it was dirt and flies, flies and dirt, everywhere. He sat in a chair with a smooth-worn cane bottom so low that his chin was just above the table. The table-cover was of greasy oilcloth. His tumbler was cloudy, unclean, and the milk was thin and sour. Thick slices of fat bacon swam in a dish of grease, blood was perceptible in the joints of the freshly killed, half-cooked chicken, and the flies swarmed.[18]

When the professor asks how these people can live this way, he is told: "They've got used to it, and so would you if your folks had been living out in this wilderness for a hundred years."[19]

Nor does Fox glamorize the appearance of his natives of the mountains. Describing a group of men gathered around the courthouse square of one little town, he writes:

A motley throng it was—in brown or gray homespun, with trousers in cowhide boots, and slouched hats with brims curved according to temperament, but with striking figures in it; the patriarch with long, white hair, shorn even with the base of the neck, and bearded only at the throat—a justice of the peace, and the sage of his district; a little mountaineer with curling black hair and beard, and dark, fine features; a grizzled giant with a head rugged enough to have been carelessly chipped from stone; a bragging candidate claiming everybody's notice;

a square-shouldered fellow surging through the crowd like a stranger; an open-faced, devil-may-care young gallant on fire with moonshine; a skulking figure with brutish mouth and shifting eyes.[20]

The hunting shirt, coonskin cap, and moccasin frequently marked the male costume, while women with their homespun or cotton dresses and their poke-bonnet headgear were typical.

That the life of the women was often harsh, Fox makes clear. They rose before the men, ate after them, and stayed up to wash the dishes and clean the kitchen after the day's work was completed; for women worked in the fields with the men. By age thirty or thirty-five, the women frequently looked old and haggard, although they might occasionally be pretty when young. Noting the striking appearance of the girl Easter in *A Mountain Europa*, Clayton observed that her countenance was "without the listless expression he had marked in other mountain women, and which, he had noticed, deadened into pathetic hopelessness later in life."[21] Elsewhere Fox wrote that "usually the women are stoop-shouldered and large waisted from working in the fields and lifting heavy weights; for the same reason their hands are large and so are their feet, for they generally go barefoot."[22] Generally, the women succumbed early to their routines and quickly became resigned to their lot in life.

Courtship rules, Fox shows, were rigid. If a man called on a girl, he was assumed to be serious. Customarily, "setting up," as courting was called, was carried on openly in the cabin before others. There were no walks alone in the woods, though occasional "woods-colts," illegitimate children, were found in the hills. No stigma attached to them, and they were treated like all others. People married young and sometimes lived together before formal marriage rites could be performed by the traveling circuit rider, as in the case of Lum Chapman and Martha Mullins in "The Lord's Own Level." A wedding was usually followed by an "infair," a dancing party, to which all the neighbors were invited. There was no wedding journey, and there were no separations except in death.

One of the more bizarre aspects of Kentucky mountain life, and one that never failed to draw the interest of outsiders (including Fox's reviewers), was the feud. Family enmities were an inheritance and usually went far back in history. They might be caused by the most trivial incident, as Fox relates in *Blue-*

grass and Rhododendron: "About thirty-five years ago two boys were playing marbles in the road along the Cumberland River—down in the Kentucky mountains. One had a patch on the seat of his trousers. The other boy made fun of it, and the boy with the patch went home and told his father. Thirty years of local war was the result. The factions fought on after they had forgotten why they had fought at all."[23] Sometimes more serious matters such as disputed boundaries, horse tradings, county court suits, or political rivalries sparked the feud. But the Civil War was the chief cause: "When it came, the river-bottoms were populated, the clans were formed. There were more slave-holders among them [the Kentucky mountaineers] than among other Southern mountaineers. For that reason, the war divided them more evenly against themselves, and set them fighting. When the war stopped elsewhere, it simply kept on with them, because they were more isolated, more evenly divided; because they were a fiercer race, and because the issue had become personal."[24]

Frequently, the feuds were led by unquestioned leaders whose audacity sometimes carried them to ludicrous lengths: "Each leader has his band of retainers. Always he arms them; usually he feeds them; sometimes he houses and clothes them, and sometimes, even, he hires them. In one local war, I remember, four dollars per day were the wages of the fighting man, and the leader on one occasion, while besieging his enemies—in the county court-house—tried to purchase a cannon, and from no other place than the State arsenal, and from no other personage than the governor himself."[25]

The feudsman had a code by which he ordinarily fought. He might assassinate his enemy from behind a tree; but, as noted earlier, he would not rob, steal, or molest the nonpartisan or traveler once the traveler's identity had been established, nor would he harm or insult women—even of the opposing clan. Indeed, women could come and go freely during times when feuds were at their height; they were inviolate. But women could be the cause of trouble if they married into the enemy camp in a feud. The Honeycutt-Hawn feud in *The Heart of the Hills* caused untold trouble to young Jason and Mavis. Jason's father, who had married a member of the opposing family of Honeycutts, had been forced to move to the other side of the mountain to escape the wrath of his own family. Mavis' father, Steve Honeycutt, had married the widowed mother of Jason; and the couple had moved to the bluegrass to work and live partly to escape the consequences of such intertribal matchings. Trouble constantly erupted in "A Cumberland Vendetta" because of the courtship of Rome Stetson and Martha Lewallen, members of feuding families.

Sometimes a feudsman would go to the West like June Tolliver's Uncle Rufe in *The Trail of the Lonesome Pine*. Such migrations usually followed a too pertinacious pursuit by the law. A slackening of interest on the part of law officers often signaled the return to the mountains of the guilty clansman. Such a return might in time spark a reopening of the feud.

Whenever the contests became too blatant and threatened the stability of the entire community, the governor of the state might send in the militia. This interference would bring a temporary order, but the feud might resume once the militia was withdrawn. And bitterly fought elections sometimes served as the justification for a resumption of feuding. Occasionally, a feud might be the sole issue in an election—members of rival families running against each other. Most mountaineers were Republicans in the 1880's and 1890's, but there could be considerable internecine fighting at the polls. There was a rivalry with the bluegrass Democrats that might bind them temporarily together, however, as in the election of 1899 when the mountaineers came down out of the hills of eastern Kentucky to Frankfort to oppose the selection of William Goebel as governor. One such mountaineer probably shot and killed Goebel, although the culprit was never apprehended. But the clash between Democrats and Republicans in this instance enabled feuding mountain groups to come together in a common cause.

Fox's stories clearly bring out the fundamentalist religious bent of the mountain people. Methodists or Baptists by inclination, and sometimes by membership, the mountain folk mixed a Calvinist strain with the grossest superstitions. Signs and omens were allied with their beliefs. The curious custom of holding annual funeral services for a deceased relative for several years after his death was not uncommon. The influence of a circuit-riding preacher, such as Sherd Raines in "A Mountain Europa" and "Preaching on Kingdom Come," could be great, even to the point of extinguishing the feuds at least temporarily. And, though the wild ruffians of Pine Mountain had little use for a Christmas tree and had never heard of Santa Claus in one of the stories of

In Happy Valley, the custom of celebrating two Noel days, New Christmas and Old Christmas, indicated some awareness, at least, of religiously inspired holidays. In "The Compact of Christopher" Fox writes that Christmas was "new Christmas" in Happy Valley: "The women give scant heed to it, and to the men it means 'a jug of liquor, a pistol in each hand, and a galloping nag.' "[26] Twelve days later, on January 6, old Christmas was celebrated: "The old folks of Happy Valley pay puritan heed to 'old Christmas.' They eat cold food and preserve a solemn demeanor on that day, and they have the pretty legend that at midnight the elders bloom and the beasts of the field and the cattle in the barn kneel, lowing and moaning."[27]

Ordinarily, however, Fox's stories reveal that the mountain people seldom let their hard faith interfere unduly with such pleasures as fiddle or banjo playing, "running sets" (dancing), drinking, and occasional card playing. Dreary or grim as life might be, the mountaineer's had its lighter moments. Saturdays and election days were occasions for the people to gather in the little towns for racing, jumpings, wrestling, and fighting "fist and skull." At other times, they could be summoned from their cabins by a blast of a horn (like that of Uncle Billy in *The Trail of the Lonesome Pine*) to an "infair" or a house-warming or a wedding celebration. *The Heart of the Hills* records one such merry scene where young Jason and Mavis "ran sets" to the mountain tunes of "Soapsuds Over the Fence," "Big Sewell Mountain," "Cattle Licking Salt," "Chicken in the Dough-Tray," and similar songs for the benefit of their bluegrass visitors. Such merriment was frequently made more boisterous by excessive drinking which was not considered immoral or vicious. Occasionally, circuit riders might inveigh against it; but, with the moonshining of liquor a veritable way of life on every hand, it was not at all incredulous that the mountaineer should have disdained any injuction to abstain from enjoying the fruits of his industry. Even the youngest boys and the women imbibed, as illustrated in the delightful little sketch "The Compact of Christopher."

Thus Fox depicts the unique qualities of an area and a people —a characteristic of local-color fiction. Whatever peculiarities the mountain folk possessed, however, were drawn from their isolation and the frontier conditions that prevailed among them into the early twentieth century. Self-reliant, independent, individualistic—these qualities grew from their isolation; sensitive, proud, equal in each other's eyes because few men owned more than a meager strip of land—these grew from the frontier condition. Fatalistic and stoic, they were not emotionally demonstrative. Few displays of affection were ordinarily evidenced. Yet they could be loyal, hospitable, and generous. Even strangers might find a hearty welcome once the initial suspicion of "furriners" had been relieved.

On the whole, Fox is most sympathetic in his portrait of the Cumberland mountaineers. Living among them or close to them, at least from the Big Stone Gap years on, he recognized their many fine qualities beneath the eccentric exterior they presented to the outsiders. Never did he treat them as curiosities, as objects of ridicule or scorn. Always he tried to know them and to present them truly as he knew them. And the mountaineers loved him for it. No writer ever went among them more freely than Fox and no one was ever held more warmly in their affections than the genteel aristocrat from the bluegrass who came to live among them in the 1890's and chose to remain close to them at the Gap.

In the final analysis, Fox's ultimate place in literature must be determined by his depiction of the Kentucky mountaineer's world of the late nineteenth century. His niche is within the local-color genre. Had he lived and written twenty, even ten, years earlier, he would fare better when literary historians evaluate the local-color movement. But he was a latecomer to regionalism who wrote only in the popular sentimental manner of his day; hence, he has only the footnote in American literary history. As the historian of the Cumberland Mountain folk, the chronicler of "our contemporary ancestors," however, John Fox has few peers. The literature of this phase of the American scene is not so rich that we can afford to discard him.

Notes and References

Preface

1. Thomas Nelson Page, "John Fox," *Scribner's Magazine*, LXVI (December, 1919), 678.

Chapter One

1. *The Little Shepherd of Kingdom Come* (New York, 1903), p. 126.

2. William Cabell Moore, "John Fox, Jr. (1862–1919)," an address delivered October 21, 1957, at the Club of Colonial Dames in Washington, D. C. MS in Fox collection, University of Kentucky Library, Lexington. (Hereafter referred to as UK coll.) Moore, a physician, was Fox's brother-in-law.

3. Fox's writings contain abundant evidence of his knowledge of botanical life. Many varieties of birds are also named in his stories.

4. James Fox to John Fox, Sr., September 28, 1879; letter in UK coll.

5. John Fox, Jr., to Horace Fox, March 21, 1880; letter in UK coll.

6. John Fox, Jr., to James Fox, October 14, 1880; letter in UK coll.

7. John Fox, Jr., to James Fox, October 24, 1880; letter in UK coll.

8. John Fox, Jr., to his mother, November 17, 1882; letter in UK coll.

9. John Fox, Jr., to his mother, November 10, 1883; letter in UK coll.

10. Moore, *loc. cit.* Fox recognized the values of experience in journalism and was probably motivated by an appreciation of the training it could give him. He wrote a Harvard classmate, for example, during these months: "I think I recognize the advantages of journalism. It is admirable training for a young fellow. He gets a great deal of practical information and learns human nature better than he could in any other way. He sees life under so many different aspects but I don't think it widens his sympathies for he regards everything merely in the light of news. My idea then is to get the good part of journalism, the training, and then to get out of it as soon as possible."

John Fox, Jr., to Micajah Fible, August 7, 1883; letter in University of Virginia Library, Charlottesville.

11. John Fox, Jr., to his mother, May 19, 1884; letter in UK coll.

12. John Fox, Jr., to his mother, July 9, 1884; letter in UK coll.

13. John Fox, Jr., to Micajah Fible, June 30, 1887; letter in University of Virginia Library, Charlottesville.

14. R. W. Gilder to John Fox, Jr., January 30, 1890; letter in UK coll.

15. James Lane Allen to John Fox, Jr., n.d.; letter in UK coll.

Chapter Two

1. Besides newspaper items, Fox had written two inconsequential sketches for the New York *Life* and *Frank Leslie's Illustrated Weekly* before "A Mountain Europa" was published in 1892.

2. *A Mountain Europa* (New York, 1899), p. 13.

3. *Ibid.*, pp. 115–16.

4. "Recent Fiction," *Nation,* LXIX (October 19, 1899), 300.

5. *A Mountain Europa,* pp. 14–15. John Kendrick Bangs, in his review of the novel for *Harper's New Monthly Magazine,* saw the historical importance of Fox's work in revealing this aspect of pioneer life. "One thinks of him rather as a delineator of historical scenes than as a mere writer of attractive fiction. . . . It is to his vivid portrayal of their characteristics that we owe our knowledge of a kind of American who but for him and Miss Murfree would have passed away unheralded and unknown. . . . In Mr. Fox's pictures of the rugged and isolated condition of the mountains we have not only the literary charm that goes with an easy, pleasing style, but an apprehension of the fact that the author is not only an author, but an authority." *Harper's New Monthly Magazine,* C (December, 1899), 168.

6. Moore, *loc. cit.*

7. *A Mountain Europa; A Cumberland Vendetta; The Last Stetson* (New York, 1910), pp. 124–25.

8. *Ibid.*, p. 126.

9. Laurence Hutton, "Literary Notes," *Harper's New Monthly Magazine,* XCI (November, 1895), 972.

10. "Novel Notes," *Bookman,* II (January, 1896), 434.

11. Hutton, *loc. cit.*

12. *A Mountain Europa; A Cumberland Vendetta; The Last Stetson,* p. 253.

13. Oddly enough, the sketch was published anonymously by *Harper's Weekly* in the back of the magazine next to the advertisements. Bill Nye and James Whitcomb Riley had used the story in platform readings and it was included in a collection of "literary masterpieces" before it was discovered that Fox was the author. Plaudits of New York literary men were then forthcoming. (Moore, *loc. cit.*)

14. *Christmas Eve on Lonesome, 'Hell-fer-Sartain' and Other Stories* (New York, 1911), p. 101. Fox intended to write a whole series of stories about Abe Shivers but never got around to doing more than the three sketches in which he appears in *Hell-fer-Sartain and Other Stories*.

15. *Ibid.*, p. 136.

16. *Ibid.*, p. 124.

17. *Ibid.*, p. 132.

18. George Merriam Hyde, "A New Crop of Dialect," *Bookman*, VI (September, 1897), 57.

19. "Hell-fer-Sartain," *Critic*, XXXI (September 11, 1897), 139.

20. Laurence Hutton, "Literary Notes," *Harper's New Monthly Magazine*, XCV (September, 1897), 648; "Notes," *Nation*, LXV (November 4, 1897), 363.

21. Charles E. L. Wingate, "A Story-teller of the Mountaineers," *Critic*, XXXI (July 24, 1897), 50.

Chapter Three

1. Fox had first met Page while working on the New York *Sun*. Later, Page read two chapters of "A Mountain Europa" to lecture audiences in Louisville before the story was published. Thus it was Page who first introduced Fox's work to the Kentucky public.

2. Thomas Nelson Page to Southern Lyceum Bureau of Louisville, Kentucky, January 22, 1894; letter in UK coll.

3. *The Kentuckians; A Knight of the Cumberland* (New York, 1910), p. 9.

4. *Ibid.*, pp. 12–13.

5. *Ibid.*, p. 13.

6. No doubt suggested by Harlan County, Kentucky. Fox may have had the celebrated Howard-Turner feud in mind in writing his story.

7. E. F. Harkins, *Little Pilgrimages Among the Men Who Have Written Famous Books* (Boston, 1903), p. 192.

8. "The Kentuckians," *Critic*, XXXII (January 1, 1898), 6.

9. John Fox, Jr., to Charles Wingate, August 26, 1897; letter in Houghton Library, Harvard University.

10. William Morton Payne, "Recent Fiction," *Dial*, XXIV (February 1, 1898), 80.

11. "The Kentuckians," *loc. cit.*; Laurence Hutton, "Literary Notes," *Harper's New Monthly Magazine*, XCVI (January, 1898), 328.

Chapter Four

1. Fox was a fellow-correspondent of Stephen Crane, Richard Harding Davis, and Frederic Remington in Cuba. Davis and Melton Prior were with him much of the time in the Orient.

2. "Chickamauga," *Harper's Weekly*, XLII (May 7, 1898), 454.

3. "A Day in Atlanta," *Harper's Weekly,* XLII (May 21, 1898), 498.

4. "Volunteers in the Blue Grass," *Harper's Weekly,* XLII (June 18, 1898), 591.

5. John Fox, Jr., to his family, June 19, 1898; letter in UK coll.

6. John Fox, Jr., to his family, June 22, 1898; letter in UK coll.

7. "With the Troops for Santiago," *Harper's Weekly,* XLII (July 16, 1898), 698.

8. *Ibid.,* p. 699.

9. "With the Rough Riders at Las Guasimas," *Harper's Weekly,* XLII (July 30, 1898), 750.

10. "Santiago and Caney," *Harper's Weekly,* XLII (August 6, 1898), 770.

11. "Truce," *Harper's Weekly,* XLII (August 13, 1898), 804.

12. San Francisco *Argonaut,* August 29, 1898; clipping in UK coll.

13. John Fox, Jr., to Charles Wingate, January 19, 1898; letter in Houghton Library, Harvard University.

14. *Crittenden* (New York, 1900), p. 33.

15. *Ibid.,* p. 19.

16. *Ibid.,* pp. 127, 128.

17. *Ibid.,* p. 145.

18. *Ibid.,* p. 231. General Jerry Carter in the novel is modelled after General Joe Wheeler, ex-Confederate cavalry commander who donned the uniform of the United States to fight in the Spanish-American War and thus helped symbolize the new unity of North and South.

19. *Ibid.,* pp. 237–38.

20. Nancy Huston Banks, "John Fox's *Crittenden,*" *Bookman,* XII (January, 1901), 485, 486.

21. Jeannette Barbour Perry, "Recent Novels Reviewed by Various Hands," *Critic,* XXXVIII (February, 1901), 164.

22. William Morton Payne, "Recent Books of Fiction," *Dial,* XXX (February 16, 1901), 110.

Chapter Five

1. *Blue-grass and Rhododendron* (New York, 1901), p. 28.

2. *Ibid.*

3. *Ibid.,* p. 40.

4. *Ibid.*

5. *Ibid.,* p. 41.

6. *Ibid.,* p. 42.

7. *Ibid.,* pp. 209–10.

8. *Ibid.,* pp. 210–11.

9. *Ibid.,* p. 210.

10. *Ibid.,* p. 224.

11. *Ibid.*

12. "Still More Novels," *Nation*, LXXIII (December 19, 1901), 477.

13. Fox wrote in 1898: "I never lost the belief that I should try someday to write fiction and about the bluegrass (the mountain work has been the accident of environment)." John Fox, Jr., to Charles Wingate, January 19, 1898; letter in Houghton Library, Harvard University.

14. *The Little Shepherd of Kingdom Come*, p. 234.

15. *Ibid.*, p. 241.

16. *Ibid.*, p. 239.

17. *Ibid.*, pp. 238–39.

18. *Ibid.*, pp. 403–04.

19. "Some Recent Books: A Distinctive Kentucky Novel," *World's Work*, VI (September, 1903), 3925.

20. Duffield Osborne, "John Fox, Jr.'s, 'The Little Shepherd of Kingdom Come'," *Bookman, XVIII* (October, 1903), 159.

21. "Recent Fiction," *Nation*, LXXVII (November 12, 1903), 390; "A Good Kentucky Story," *Independent*, LV (October 15, 1903), 2466.

22. Frank Luther Mott, *Golden Multitudes* (New York, 1947), p. 312. Mott writes, "The book was published by Scribners in 1903 and was a success from the first. . . . A questionnaire to librarians as late as 1932 showed that *The Little Shepherd*, as well as its author's other great hit,*The Trail of the Lonesome Pine*, were among the older books in chief demand at the public libraries. It has had a total sale of about 1,225,000 copies." (p. 214). Since the book is still in print, it has now well exceeded this total.

23. *Ibid.*, p. 214.

24. *The Little Shepherd of Kingdom Come*, p. 126.

25. *Ibid.*, p. 129.

26. *Christmas Eve on Lonesome, 'Hell-fer-Sartain' and Other Stories*, pp. 56, 57.

27. Page, p. 676. *Christmas Eve on Lonesome and Other Stories* was dedicated to Page.

Chapter Six

1. John Fox, Jr., to James Fox, July 22, 1903; letter in UK coll.

2. John Fox, Jr., to his mother, August 6, 1903; letter in UK coll.

3. John Fox, Jr., to his mother, January 14, 1904; letter in UK coll. The family, of course, did not choose to return then or ever.

4. John Fox, Jr., to his mother, February 21, 1904; letter in UK coll.

5. John Fox, Jr., to his mother, March 4, 1904; letter in UK coll.

6. *Following the Sun-Flag* (New York, 1905), p. 9.

7. John Fox, Jr., to his family, March 20, 1904; letter in UK coll.

8. John Fox, Jr., to his mother, May 7, 1904; letter in UK coll.

9. John Fox, Jr., to his mother, May 23, 1904; letter in UK coll.

10. John Fox, Jr., to his mother, August 15, 1904; letter in UK coll.

11. *Following the Sun-Flag,* p. 157.

12. *Ibid.,* p. 188.

13. *Ibid.,* pp. 188–89.

14. New York *Times,* May 6, 1905, p. 10; *Spectator,* XCV (August 8, 1905), 51; "Notes," *Nation,* LXXXI (July 13, 1905), 42; William Elliot Griffis, "Books on the Far East," *Critic,* XLVII (September, 1905), 264; Wallace Rice, "Echoes from the Eastern Struggle," *Dial,* XXXVIII (June 16, 1905), 416.

15. *Following the Sun-Flag,* p. x.

Chapter Seven

1. *A Knight of the Cumberland* (New York, 1906), p. 4.

2. *Ibid.,* p. 29.

3. Agnes Repplier, "A Sheaf of Autumn Fiction," *Outlook,* XC (November 28, 1908), 701.

4. *The Trail of the Lonesome Pine* (New York, 1908), p. 181.

5. *Ibid.,* pp. 97–98. The Honorable Sam Budd, a Kentucky state senator, is another of several Fox characters who appear in more than one story.

6. *Ibid.,* p. 97.

7. *Ibid.,* pp. 201–02.

8. *Ibid.,* pp. 415, 416.

9. Judd Tolliver remarks to his daughter when Hale first suggests her departure from Lonesome Cove, "So you ain't good enough fer him jest as ye air—air ye? He's got to make ye all over agin—so's you'll be fitten fer him." (*Ibid.,* p. 201.) Apparently she was "fitten" by the end of the story.

10. "A Strong, Human, American Love Story," *Review of Reviews,* XXXVIII (November, 1908), 632.

11. "Comment on Current Books," *Outlook,* XC (October 17, 1908), 361.

12. Ward Clark, "Mr. Fox's 'The Trail of the Lonesome Pine'," *Bookman,* XXVIII (December, 1908), 364.

13. "Current Fiction," *Nation,* LXXXVII (November 12, 1908), 466.

14. "Appalachian Fiction," *Independent,* LXV (November 12, 1908), 1121; New York *Times,* October 17, 1908, p. 570.

15. Mott, p. 312.

16. Oliver E. Fox, brother of the novelist, wanted "The Trail of the Lonesome Pine" to follow a route leading from the mountains to the bluegrass in Kentucky, not paralleling the mountains as Virginia had done in its highway markings. This would seem more appropriate, but

the state of Kentucky has never designated a "Trail of the Lonesome
Pine" highway. (Oliver E. Fox, "The Trail of the Lonesome Pine: A
Description of the Setting for John Fox, Jr.'s Romantic Story and a
Plea for Authentic Road Markings," Winchester [Kentucky] *Sun,* April
9, 13, 23, 27, 1936; clippings in UK coll.)

17. Joe Creason, "Friend to the Mountaineer," Louisville *Courier-
Journal,* June 12, 1949, magazine section; clipping in John Fox, Jr..
Memorial Library Room, Duncan Tavern, Paris, Kentucky.

18. Fox's sister, Elizabeth (Mrs. Cabell Moore), told me in June,
1965, that the novel was inspired by a mining engineer named James
Hodge who brought a little eight or nine-year-old girl out of the mountains to Big Stone Gap to attend school.

19. *The Trail of the Lonesome Pine,* p. 6.

20. *Ibid.,* pp. 5–6.

21. "On The Trail of the Lonesome Pine," *Scribner's Magazine,*
XLVIII (October, 1910), 417.

Chapter Eight

1. Fox dedicated *The Trail of the Lonesome Pine* to Fritzi Scheff.
Arthur N. Kruger has noted some similarities between Fritzi and June
Tolliver of the novel. Both loved flowers and were talented singers, for
example. (Arthur N. Kruger, "The Life and Work of John Fox, Jr.,"
unpublished Ph.D. thesis, Louisiana State University, 1941.)

2. "On Horseback to Kingdom Come," *Scribner's Magazine,* XLVIII
(August, 1910), 175.

3. *Ibid.,* p. 176.

4. *Ibid.,* p. 178.

5. "On the Road to Hell-fer-Sartain," *Scribner's Magazine,* LXVIII
(September, 1910), 350.

6. Thomas D. Clark, *A History of Kentucky* (New York, 1937), p.
615.

7. Frederic Taber Cooper, "Big Moments in Fiction and Some
Recent Novels," *Bookman,* XXXVII (August, 1913), 665.

8. *The Heart of the Hills* (New York, 1913), pp. 264–65.

9. "A Few of the Season's Novels," *Review of Reviews,* XLVII
(June, 1913), 762.

10. "The New Books," *Outlook,* CIII (March 29, 1913), 733.

11. "Other Novels of the Season," *Literary Digest,* XLVI (April 5,
1913), 780.

12. Cooper, *loc. cit.*

13. "The New Books," *Independent,* LXXIV (May 29, 1913), 1203.

14. "Current Fiction," *Nation,* XCVI (May 29, 1913), 548.

15. William Morton Payne, "Recent Fiction," *Dial,* LIV (June 1,
1913), 464.

16. New York *Times,* March 23, 1913, p. 155.

Chapter Nine

1. On one of his fishing excursions along the gulf coast of Florida, Fox incurred the displeasure of the Audubon Society of the United States by violating the Federal Migratory Bird Law. "Birds were always flying around the boat—gulls, men-of-war, pelicans—and when we weren't fishing we were potting at them with a Winchester 22," Fox wrote of the experience. ("Tarpon-fishing at Boca Grande," *Scribner's Magazine,* LIX [February, 1916] 213.) Later, he sent a letter of apology and regret to the Society and offered his assurance that it would never happen again.

2. *In Happy Valley* (New York, 1917), pp. 56–57.

3. *Ibid.,* p. 62.

4. *Ibid.,* pp. 188–89.

5. *Ibid.,* p. 200.

6. "Notes on New Fiction," *Dial,* LXIII (November 8, 1917), 464.

7. H. W. Boynton, "A Stroll Through the Fair of Fiction," *Bookman, XLVI* (November, 1917), 341.

8. "Recent Publications," *New Republic,* XIII (November 10, 1917), 56.

9. E. P. Wyckoff, "Review of 'In Happy Valley'," *Publisher's Weekly,* XCII (October 20, 1917), 1376.

10. Kruger reports that Fox practically stopped writing for a time after his divorce from Fritzi Scheff and that he fell into heavy drinking habits which gradually undermined his health. Certainly he grew more worldly, more interested in social pleasures, and less interested in literature after about 1908. (Kruger, *loc. cit.*)

11. Serial publication in *Scribner's* (January to July, 1920) preceded the book.

12. *Erskine Dale—Pioneer* (New York, 1920), pp. 113–14.

13. "Among the Novels," *Outlook,* CXXVI (October 20, 1920), 333.

14. New York *Times,* Book Review and Magazine, October 17, 1920, p. 10.

15. "Review of *Erskine Dale," Catholic World,* CXII (January, 1921), 552.

16. "Fox's 'Erskine Dale'," *Cleveland* (December, 1920), 6.

17. Moore, *loc. cit.* Fox's sister Minnie is given as the authority for these words that were probably written by Fox at the time of his father's death. On September 3, 1939, twenty years after the author's death, a memorial plaque was unveiled at the site of Fox's birthplace and childhood home, Stony Point, on the Winchester Pike east of Paris, Kentucky. On October 24, 1950, the John Fox, Jr., Memorial Library Room was dedicated at the Duncan Tavern Historic Center in Paris. These are two manifestations of Kentucky's effort to honor the popular writer who was her native son.

Chapter Ten

1. Page, pp. 681, 680.

2. Among the few writers Fox did know well were Thomas Nelson Page, James Lane Allen, Richard Harding Davis, Robert Burns Wilson, and Madison Cawein. Page wrote of Fox: "Few writers have paid less court to those who are supposed to be the judges in the field of modern literature—'the Literati.' He was frankly bored by the conventionality of the ordinary literary life and evaded it with joyous satisfaction." (Page, p. 678.)

3. Page, p. 683.

4. Wilma Stokely has written of the "purple prose and pathetic fallacies" of Mary Murfree. "She was provincial rather than regional—she knew the mountains only from summer visits to the resorts." (Wilma D. Stokely, "The Literature of the Southern Appalachian Mountains," *Mountain Life and Work,* XL [Winter, 1964], 7.) Fox certainly could match Miss Murfree in the purple prose and pathetic fallacies. Unlike her, however, he did know the mountaineers and their life from living among them.

5. Quoted from *Harper's Weekly* in promotional pamphlet on Fox published by Southern Lyceum Bureau, UK coll.

6. John Patterson, "John Fox," in *Library of Southern Literature,* Vol. IV (Atlanta, 1907), p. 1684.

7. *Blue-grass and Rhododendron,* pp. 6–7.

8. Occasionally Fox does allow a bluegrass type to remain in the mountains—for example, Hale in *The Trail of the Lonesome Pine* and St. Hilda in *The Heart of the Hills.*

9. In *The Heart of the Hills,* Jason Hawn hears a passing lecturer at the university discuss the mountain people and refer to them as "our contemporary ancestors." (*The Heart of the Hills,* p. 202.) Such a lecturer could have been Fox himself.

10. *Blue-grass and Rhododendron,* pp. 46–47.

11. *Ibid.,* pp. 47–48. As an amateur musician, Fox had an interest in mountaineer folk-songs, which he correctly considered trans-Atlantic remnants of Scotch, Irish, and English origins. The mountaineer's speech touched a remote past too. Fox noted approximately two hundred words that went back in meaning or pronunciation to Chaucer's time (for example, *afeered, afore, axe, holp, crope, clomb, peert, cryke, fer, heepe, hit, lepte,* and *pore*). Yet nowhere did he find the mountaineer's usage sustained or consistent enough to be called a dialect. "To writers of mountain stories the temptation seems quite irresistible to use more peculiar words in one story than can be gathered from the people in a month." (*Ibid.,* p. 15.)

12. *Ibid.,* p. 49.

13. *Ibid.,* pp. 52, 53.

14. *Ibid.,* p. 53.

15. *Ibid.*

16. *The Little Shepherd of Kingdom Come,* p. 2.

17. *In Happy Valley,* pp. 148–49.

18. *Ibid.,* pp. 161–62.

19. *Ibid.,* p. 163.

20. *A Mountain Europa, A Cumberland Vendetta, The Last Stetson,* pp. 184–85.

21. *A Mountain Europa,* p. 9.

22. *Blue-grass and Rhododendron,* p. 33.

23. *Ibid.,* p. 39.

24. *Ibid.,* p. 41.

25. *Ibid.,* p. 40.

26. *In Happy Valley,* p. 35.

27. *Ibid.,* p. 36.

Selected Bibliography

PRIMARY SOURCES

I. *Manuscript Collections*

Duncan Tavern Historic Center, Paris, Kentucky:
Fox brochures from Southern Lyceum Bureau
Manuscript of *The Trail of the Lonesome Pine*
Scrapbooks of newspaper clippings
Louisville Free Public Library, Louisville, Kentucky:
"Kentucky Authors Scrapbook"
Miscellaneous letters of John Fox, Jr., in library collections of Allegheny College, Duke University, Harvard University, Indiana University, Loyola University, New York Public Library, Randolph-Macon Woman's College, and Yale University.
University of Kentucky Library, Lexington:
Diaries of John Fox, Sr.
Drafts of stories, novels, and public lectures
"John Fox, Jr. (1862-1919)" by William Cabell Moore, typescript of an address delivered October 21, 1957, at the Club of Colonial Dames, Washington, D.C.
Letters of Fox family, 1852-1920
Notebooks and papers from Harvard College days
Notebooks from Russo-Japanese War
Scrapbooks of newspaper clippings, letters from publishers and editors, letters from readers
University of Virginia Library, Charlottesville:
Letters from John Fox, Jr., to Micajah Fible, 1883-1889, assembled by Betty Fible Martin

II. *Published Works of John Fox, Jr.*

1. Books (First Editions Only):

Blue-grass and Rhododendron. New York: Charles Scribner's Sons, 1901.

Christmas Eve on Lonesome and Other Stories. New York: Charles Scribner's Sons, 1904.

Crittenden. New York: Charles Scribner's Sons, 1900.

A Cumberland Vendetta and Other Stories. New York: Harper & Brothers, 1895.

Erskine Dale—Pioneer. New York: Charles Scribner's Sons, 1920.

Following the Sun Flag. New York: Charles Scribner's Sons, 1905.

The Heart of the Hills. New York: Charles Scribner's Sons, 1913.

Hell-fer-Sartain and Other Stories. New York: Harper & Brothers, 1897.

In Happy Valley. New York: Charles Scribner's Sons, 1917.

The Kentuckians. New York: Harper & Brothers, 1897.

A Knight of the Cumberland. New York: Charles Scribner's Sons, 1906.

The Little Shepherd of Kingdom Come. New York: Charles Scribner's Sons, 1903.

A Mountain Europa. New York: Harper & Brothers, 1899.

The Trail of the Lonesome Pine. New York: Charles Scribner's Sons, 1908.

2. Magazine Articles and Stories:

"After Br'er Rabbit in the Blue-grass," *Century,* LIII (November, 1896), 97–103.

"Angel from Viper," *Scribner's Magazine,* LXI (May, 1917), 539–42.

"Army of the Callahan," *Scribner's Magazine,* XXXII (July, 1902), 73–86.

"Backward Trail of the Saxon," *Scribner's Magazine,* XXXVII (March, 1905), 274–80.

"Battle-Prayer of Parson Small," *Scribner's Magazine,* LXI (April, 1917), 404–7.

"Br'er Coon in Old Kentucky," *Century,* LV (February, 1898), 594–601.

"Chickamauga," *Harper's Weekly,* XLII (May 7–14, June 11, 1898), 454, 475, 574–5.

"Christmas Eve on Lonesome," *Ladies Home Journal,* XIX (December, 1901), 8.

"Christmas for Big Ame," *Scribner's Magazine,* XLVIII (December, 1910), 690–5.

"Christmas Night With Satan," *Scribner's Magazine,* XXXIV (December, 1903), 673–82.

"Christmas Tree on Pigeon," *Collier's,* XLIV (December 11, 1909), 10–11.

"Compact of Christopher," *Scribner's Magazine,* LXI (February, 1917), 133–6.

"Courtin' on Cutshin," *Harper's Weekly,* XXXIX (December 21, 1895), 1213.

"Courtship of Allaphair," *Scribner's Magazine,* LXI (January, 1917), 1–7.

"A Cumberland Vendetta," *Century,* XLVIII (June–August, 1894), 163–78, 366–73, 496–505.

"A Day in Atlanta," *Harper's Weekly,* XLII (May 21, 1898), 498.

"Down the Kentucky on a Raft," *Scribner's Magazine,* XXVII (June, 1900), 664–69.

"Erskine Dale—Pioneer," *Scribner's Magazine,* LXVII (January–June, 1920), 9–17, 177–86, 257–65, 459–69, 539–48, 729–38; LXVIII (July, 1920), 1–11.

"Fox-Hunting in Kentucky," *Century,* L (August, 1895), 620–8.

"Goddess of Happy Valley," *Scribner's Magazine,* LXII (October, 1917), 411–19.

"Grayson's Baby," *Harper's Weekly,* XL (May 9, 1896), 467.

"Hanging of Talton Hall," *Outing,* XXXIX (October, 1901), 39–45.

"Hardships of the Campaign," *Scribner's Magazine,* XXXVI (July, 1904), 38–45.

"The Heart of the Hills," *Scribner's Magazine,* LI (April–June, 1912), 384–94, 561–70, 691–701; LII (July–December, 1912), 52–63, 181–90, 341–9, 492–500, 570–78, 697–706; LIII (January–March, 1913), 102–14, 252–62, 321–33.

"The Kentuckians," *Harper's Monthly,* XCV (July–October, 1897), 242–53, 357–73, 535–46, 763–71.

"A Knight of the Cumberland," *Scribner's Magazine,* XL (September–November, 1906), 257–63, 452–59, 546–60.

"The Last Stetson," *Harper's Weekly,* XXXIX (June 29, 1895), 608–09.

"The Little Shepherd of Kingdom Come," *Scribner's Magazine,* XXXIII (January–June, 1903), 85–100, 219–36, 326–40, 467–81, 588–603, 711–27; XXXIV (July–August, 1903), 50–65, 183–96.

"Lord's Own Level," *Scribner's Magazine,* LXI (March, 1917), 273–76.

"Making for Manchuria," *Scribner's Magazine,* XXIV (December, 1904), 689–95.

"Man-hunting in the Pound," *Outing,* XXXVI (July, 1900), 344–50.

"Marquise of Queensberry," *Scribner's Magazine,* LXII (September, 1917), 273–79.

"Message in the Sand," *Harper's Weekly,* XL (June 20, 1896), 611.

"A Mountain Europa," *Century,* XLIV (September–October, 1892), 760–75, 846–58.

"On Horseback to Kingdom Come," *Scribner's Magazine,* XLVIII (August, 1910), 175–86.

"On the Road to Hell-fer-Sartain," *Scribner's Magazine,* XLVIII (September, 1910), 350–61.

"On the Trail of the Lonesome Pine," *Scribner's Magazine,* XLVIII (October, 1910), 417–29.

"On the War-Dragon's Trail," *Scribner's Magazine,* XXXVII (January, 1905), 54–9.

"On Trial for His Life," *Current Literature,* XXXV (November, 1903), 575–79.

"The Passing of Abraham Shivers," *Century,* LII (June, 1896), 320.

"Pope of the Big Sandy," *Scribner's Magazine,* LXI (June, 1917), 669–72.

"Preachin' on Kingdom-Come," *Harper's Weekly,* XL (September 5, 1896), 874.

"Santiago and Caney," *Harper's Weekly,* XLII (July 23–August 6, 1898), 724, 744, 770.

"The Senator's Last Trade," *Harper's Weekly,* XL (May 2, 1896), 446.

"The Southern Mountaineer," *Scribner's Magazine,* XXIX (April–May, 1901), 387–99, 556–70.

"Tarpon-Fishing at Boca Grande," *Scribner's Magazine,* LIX (February, 1916), 213–17.

"Through the Bad Bend," *Harper's Weekly,* XLI (December 18, 1897), 1257.

"Through the Gap," *Harper's Weekly,* XL (January 11, 1896), 39.

"To the Breaks of Sandy," *Scribner's Magazine,* XXVIII (September, 1900), 340–49.

"The Trail of the Lonesome Pine," *Scribner's Magazine,* XLIII (January–June, 1908), 33–46, 157–68, 291–306, 421–33, 597–608, 657–68; XLIV (July–November, 1908), 89–100, 229–40, 314–22, 469–78, 565–74.

"Trail of the Saxon," *Scribner's Magazine,* XXXV (June, 1904), 658–61.

"Truce," *Harper's Weekly,* XLII (August 13, 1898), 802–4.

"Volunteers in the Blue Grass," *Harper's Weekly,* XLII (June
    18, 1898), 591.
"White Slaves of Haicheng," *Scribner's Magazine,* XXXVII
    (February, 1905), 196–203.
"With the Rough Riders at Las Guasimas," *Harper's Weekly,*
    XLII (July 30, 1898), 750–51.
"With the Troops for Santiago," *Harper's Weekly,* XLII (July
    16, 1898), 698–70.

SECONDARY SOURCES

Appreciations of Richard Harding Davis. New York: Charles Scrib-
    ner's Sons, 1917. Contains introduction Fox wrote for Davis' novel
    The White Mice in 1916.
BLANCK, JACOB. *Bibliography of American Literature.* Vol. III. New
    Haven: Yale University Press, 1959. The most detailed listing of
    all editions of Fox's books.
BOGER, LOUISE C. *The Southern Mountaineer in Literature: An Anno-
    tated Bibliography.* Morgantown: West Virginia University Li-
    brary, 1964. Lists several Fox titles.
BURRAGE, WALTER L. *Class of 1883, Harvard College, Thirtieth Anni-
    versary: 1883–1913.* Boston: E. O. Cockayne, 1913. Statement of
    Fox's accomplishments in fiction to date.
CANTRELL, CLYDE H. and WALTON R. PATRICK. *Southern Literary
    Culture: A Bibliography of Masters' and Doctors' Theses.* Tusca-
    loosa: University of Alabama Press, 1955. Lists one doctoral dis-
    sertation (Kruger's) and four master's theses devoted exclusively
    to Fox; twenty-two other listed theses have some considerations of
    Fox as parts of larger topics.
CLARK, THOMAS D. *A History of Kentucky.* New York: Prentice-Hall,
    Inc., 1937. Useful for describing Goebel affair and Tobacco War
    discussed by Fox in *The Heart of the Hills.*
CREASON, JOE. "The Lonesome Pine's Gone from the Trail," *Courier-
    Journal Magazine* [Louisville, Kentucky], February 22, 1961, p. 16.
    Other articles by the same author were published in the *Courier-
    Journal Magazine* on February 22, 1948, June 12, 1949, Novem-
    ber 12, 1950, and July 9, 1957. All are primarily concerned with
    the locale of Fox's work.
FOX, MINNIE. "Observations of Himself Written by John Fox, Jr.,"
    The Kentuckian-Citizen [Paris, Kentucky], September 1, 1939, sec.
    1, p. 1; sec. 2, p. 7; sec. 3, p. 7. A sister's compilation from his
    notebooks.
FOX, OLIVER E. "The Trail of the Lonesome Pine. A Description of
    the Setting for John Fox, Jr.'s Romantic Story. A Plea for Authen-
    tic Road Markings," Winchester [Kentucky] *Sun,* April 9, 13, 23,
    27, 1936; clipping in scrapbook, John Fox, Jr., Memorial Library

Room, Duncan Tavern Historic Center, Paris, Kentucky. Identifies locale of Fox's work.

GREEN, CLAUD B. "The Rise and Fall of Local Color in Southern Literature," *Mississippi Quarterly,* XVIII (Winter, 1965–66), 1–6. Although no specific mention is made of Fox, the major thesis of this discussion applies directly to him: "The nineteenth century writers of Southern fiction, particularly the local colorists, were writing social history at a time before many of the professional historians were particularly interested in that genre. That almost invariably these fictionalized social studies also narrated a romantic love story is more a commentary on the literary climate of the times than it is on the merit of the work."

GREEN, HAROLD E. *Towering Pines, the Life of John Fox, Jr.* Boston: Meador Publishing Company, 1943. The only book-length biography of Fox in print. Largely unreliable because Green confuses the author with another John Fox, Jr. Most of the book consists of quotations from Fox's novels and stories.

HARKINS, EDWARD F. *Little Pilgrimages Among the Men Who Have Written Famous Books.* Boston: L. C. Page & Company, 1903. Interesting discussion of Fox, the man, his personality and eccentricities. Time has not substantiated the high praise of Fox, the writer.

HYDE, FREDERIC G. "American Literature and the Spanish-American War: A Study of the Work of Crane, Norris, Fox, and Richard Harding Davis." Unpublished doctoral dissertation, University of Pennsylvania, 1963. Finds Fox's style altered, largely for the worse, by his war experience "in that the melodramatic effects he employed in his war dispatches carried over into his post-war novels."

"John Fox, Jr. and His Kentucky," *Nation,* CIX (July 19, 1919), 72–73. Judicious summing-up of Fox's contribution to literature that notes his accurate knowledge of mountaineer life and the conventionality and sentimentality of his ideas and art. "Sugar spoils sooner than salt in literature."

"John Fox, Jr." *National Cyclopaedia of American Biography,* XIV, 90. Brief sketch with some inaccuracies (error in birth date and in publication dates for some of Fox's books).

KRUGER, ARTHUR N. "The Life and Works of John Fox, Jr." Unpublished doctoral dissertation, Louisiana State University, 1941. The most complete study available.

KUNITZ, STANLEY J., ed. *Authors Today and Yesterday.* New York: H. W. Wilson Company, 1934. Contains sketchy but accurate biographical article on Fox.

MARCOSSON, ISAAC F. "The South in Fiction," *Bookman,* XXXII (December, 1910), 363–69. Includes discussion of Fox's treatment of the mountain locale and identifies settings for some of his stories.

MOORE, ELIZABETH FOX. *John Fox, Jr.—Personal and Family Letters.*

Lexington: University of Kentucky Library Associates, 1953. Published in a limited edition to correct misinformation in Green's biography. Mrs. Moore is the author's sister.

New York *Times,* July 9, 1919, p. 13. Obituary that contains biographical summary.

NYE, FRANK WILSON. *Bill Nye: His Own Life Story.* New York: The Century Company, 1926. Contains account of a lecture and reading trip made with Fox.

OSBORN, SCOTT C. "A Study and Contrast of the Kentucky Mountaineer and the Blue Grass Aristocrat in the Works of John Fox, Jr." Unpublished master's thesis, University of Kentucky, 1939. Excellent study of one important aspect of Fox's writing.

PAGE, ROSEWELL. *Thomas Nelson Page: A Memoir of a Virginia Gentleman.* New York: Charles Scribner's Sons, 1923. Cites Page's friendship with Fox.

PAGE, THOMAS NELSON. "John Fox," *Scribner's Magazine,* LXVI (December, 1919), 674–83. Informative though eulogistic.

PATTERSON, JOHN. "John Fox," *Library of Southern Literature,* IV, 1683–88. Author knew Fox as a youth. Valuable account of early life with less useful discussion of the fiction.

QUINN, ARTHUR HOBSON. *American Fiction: An Historical and Critical Survey.* New York: D. Appleton-Century Company, 1936. Treats Fox as the youngest and least important of a group of writers who wrote of "place and race in American fiction" beginning with the 1870's.

RUTHERFORD, MILDRED L. *The South in History and Literature.* Atlanta: The Franklin-Turner Company, 1907. A pro-South account that inflates Fox's importance.

STOKELY, WILMA D. "The Literature of the Southern Appalachian Mountains," *Mountain Life and Work,* XL (Winter, 1964), 7–18. No mention of Fox, but a useful article for placing his work in perspective.

THOMPSON, LAWRENCE S. and ALGERNON D. THOMPSON. *The Kentucky Novel.* Lexington: University of Kentucky Press, 1953. An annotated bibliography that includes some of Fox's work.

TITUS, WARREN I. "John Fox, Jr.," *American Literary Realism, 1870–1910,* I (Summer, 1968), 5–8. Brief bibliographical essay including history of Fox criticism, editions, reprints, published manuscript material, manuscript collections, and areas needing further attention.

TOWNSEND, JOHN W. *Kentucky in American Letters.* Cedar Rapids, Iowa: The Torch Press, 1913. Remarkably well balanced estimate of Fox. "That he is a wonderful maker of short stories in the mountain dialect is certain; but that he is a great novelist is yet to be established." Considers *Hell-fer-Sartain and Other Stories* his best work and reprints "The Christmas Tree on Pigeon."

WADE, JOHN D. "John Fox," *Dictionary of American Biography*, VI, 570. Brief but accurate biographical sketch.

WAGENKNECHT, EDWARD. *Cavalcade of the American Novel*. New York: Henry Holt and Company, 1952. One of the few more recent studies of American fiction that give Fox anything more than an occasional footnote. Discusses *The Little Shepherd of Kingdom Come* and *The Trail of the Lonesome Pine* as "by common consent" his best.

"When John Fox Danced His Last Dance," *Literary Digest*, LXXXVII (October 17, 1925), 70–71. Account of a dance with Berela, "the queen of the Forty-nine" (a carnival tent show), two nights before he died. Refers to the "tragedy stalking his last days" when he desperately wanted to write a classic historical novel.

WINGATE, CHARLES E. "A Story-teller of the Mountaineers," *Critic*, XXXI (July 24, 1897), 50. Early article that predicts Fox's future popular fame.

Index

operations at Jellico, Tennessee, 23-24; move to Big Stone Gap, Virginia, 37-39; public reading and lectures, 39-40; reporter in Japan and Manchuria, 78-81; Spanish-American War reporter, 46-51; style and technique in writing, 122-24; subjects of his writing, 124-35; ultimate place in literature, 136

WRITINGS OF: